And Save $1000s!

- The facts about RV prices.

- Suggested retail prices: Are they real?

- When to buy a used RV instead of a new one.

- How to buy a used RV.

- How and where to find bargains.

- How to negotiate price and get the best deal on an RV.

- How to save money by avoiding RV price increases.

ISBN 0-937877-38-7

- Questions to ask about RV brands.

How to Buy an RV
And Save $1000s!
Third Edition
by Don Wright

Copyright® 2001 by Cottage Publications, Inc.

Printed in the United States of America

How to Buy an RV (And Save $1000s)
First Edition 1994
Second Edition 1996

ISBN 0-937877-38-7

Cottage Publications, Inc.
24396 Pleasant View Drive
Elkhart, IN 46517
Phone 800/272-5518
www.cottagepub.com
E-mail:campguide@msn.com

Contents

INTRODUCTION

For many years, America's RV enthusiast magazines have published articles that provide prospective RV buyers with a common-sense formula on how to decide which type and size RVs they should consider purchasing.

This book does not do that!

It also does not talk much about floorplans, weight ratings and tow vehicles. It assumes you have already waded through all those magazine articles and are now ready for some practical, straightforward shopping advice. It assumes you have already determined how much money you can spend for your RV and that you have narrowed your choices to a travel trailer, fifth-wheel, motorhome, folding camping trailer, van camper or pickup camper. It assumes you have at least a general idea of the floorplan that will best fit your needs, that you already have made a decision about a tow vehicle, that you've educated yourself about gear ratios, weight ratings, transmission coolers, hitches, tires and batteries.

This book will tell you things you need to know that the RV magazines avoid discussing: RV prices, dealer markups, when to buy a used versus a new RV, how to determine which brands to avoid, how to find bargains and how to dicker with dealers for the best price possible.

We'll lead you, step by step, on an RV shopping expedition and warn you about the pitfalls you're likely to encounter along the way. No matter whether you are a veteran RV owner or a first-time buyer, we'll help you make decisions that will save you time, reduce your costs and clear up your confusion about the RV-purchasing process.

Who, you might ask, is this guy who claims to be able to do all that?

Well, let me warn you: This book is *not* a result of my being an RV enthusiast for nearly 40 years, although I cringe to realize that I *have* been towing trailers that long. Rather, it is, in part, a consequence of the 20 years I spent writing about the RV industry and testing hundreds of trailers, motorhomes, van campers, pickup campers and tow vehicles. More than that, the "insider" information contained in it was learned, in large measure, during the seven years I was employed in market research by two of the premiere RV manufacturers in America -- Holiday Rambler Corporation and Newmar Corporation -- then later in a product research consultant capacity for various RV manufacturers.

In writing that, I just realized myself that research on this book actually began on that day in 1960 when I wrote my first freelance article for *Trailer Life* magazine. Between then and now, I camped at every opportunity for 15 years when I wasn't behind my Ohio newspaper editor's desk; spent nearly 10 years as the Midwest Editor of *Trailer Life's* family of magazines; researched and wrote more than 2,000 articles on camping, RVs and the RV industry; published a national camping magazine; founded the RV industry's first trade newsletter and the first national newsletter for RV travelers; authored six books about camping; served in vice president positions at two RV companies; took on the job of publishing *Camping Today* magazine for what used to be called the National Campers & Hikers Association (now Family Campers & RVers), and provided the editorial content for an RV-enthusiast website on the Internet.

And in my *spare* time, I went **CAMPING**!

All the while, I've been more than a little bothered by the fact that *NO ONE* was telling prospective RV buyers the full dope on how to purchase a recreational vehicle. Sure, they were being told how to *CHOOSE* one, but that's not the same as telling how to *BUY* one.

I had to do it. Something inside me wouldn't let me *not* do it.

Because in my twisted, slightly off-track way of thinking, I really believe that if people learn *how* to buy an RV at the best possible price, they're more likely to buy one and enjoy it, and then they'll tell other people how much fun they're having in it so that eventually, there'll be a whole lot more of us out there tooling around the country with our RVs, enjoying a special lifestyle that -- unfortunately -- too many of the people who build and sell RVs know nothing about!

So here it is. I hope you enjoy it and gain something from reading it.

And if you pass me on the road on your way to somewhere in your new rig, be sure to wave or honk, and I'll do the same because we're the same, you and me, and we really know how to live!

1
THE FACTS ABOUT RV PRICES

Contrary to popular belief, recreational vehicle prices are not necessarily related directly to an RV's length, its type of construction and its standard or optional equipment. The primary determining factor of an RV's price is *PROFIT* -- the amount of profit the manufacturer and dealer intend to earn from building and selling the product.

No other single factor is even remotely as important as the amount of profit built into the price of a recreational vehicle.

Typically, an RV dealership marks up each of its products between 30% and 40%, thereby earning gross profits of between 23% and 29%.

To illustrate that, let's look at a typical scenario involving one of today's most popular brands of low-cost travel trailers and Class C motorhomes. The trailer has a retail price of $15,000. It has been marked up 30% by the dealer, earning him a profit of $3,462, a gross margin of 23%. The dealer paid $11,358 for the trailer.

The 29-foot mini-motorhome retails for $40,900, marked up 30% from the $31,461 it cost the dealer. The dealer's profit is $9,439, a gross margin of 23%.

The picture changes when higher-priced RVs are considered. For example, a popular brand of mid-priced Class A motorhome has a retail price tag of $84,000. The dealer paid $60,000 for it, meaning he will earn a profit of $24,000 if he sells the coach for its full retail price after marking it up 40% and assigning a gross margin of 29%.

Prior to about 1980, most RV prices were generally linked to a unit's length and its construction in the minds of both consumers and those in the RV industry who built them and sold them. Then, the rule of thumb was that a low-priced Class A motorhome should be retail-priced at $1,000 per foot. That meant a typical entry-level coach 28 feet long could be sold by dealers for about $28,000. When you consider that the wholesale price of the motorhome was $20,000, you can see that dealers in those days had the potential for earning excellent profits, proportionately speaking, but even so, their per-unit dollar profit was considerably less than it is today.

THE PRICES ESCALATED

As we moved into the early 1980s, price was still associated with length, but on a different level. When raw motorhome chassis costs escalated from $6,000 to more than $12,000, the $1,000-per-foot rule evolved until it was no longer applied to the *retail* price of the coach, but to its *wholesale* price. Thus, the same entry-level 28-foot Class A suddenly cost the dealer $28,000, and his asking retail price for it was $39,000. Both dealers and retail customers suffered from severe sticker shock, and that was when the entire industry began to hear complaints that RVs were "no longer affordable."

Meanwhile, RV costs through the 1970s were also directly associated with the type and quality of the RV brand's construction. A wood-frame RV was the least expensive; an aluminum-frame unit was the most expensive. Rounded, radiused corners cost more to build and therefore were used only on the highest priced models. Laminated-panel sidewalls with fiberglass exterior skin also were fairly expensive, but the cost could be justified on motorized RVs, if not on towables. Only towables in the mid-price range or higher could feature molded fiberglass front and rear caps.

Clearly, RV pricing was strictly structured according to length, type of construction, component costs and even aerodynamics. Entry-level RVs were small, square and economically built; luxury-class RVs were large, more aerodynamic and built with the most expensive materials and techniques available.

ARRIVAL OF THE LIGHTWEIGHTS

All that changed with the energy crunch and the economic downturn that started during the spring of 1979. Aerodynamic, lightweight RVs were thought to be the products of the future. Large RVs suddenly became regarded as gas-guzzlers and dinosaurs. Among RV manufacturers, there was a panicked rush toward high-tech construction methods and exotic, lightweight materials. "Downsizing" became the watch-word of the early 1980s, and an RV's retail price was considered less important than its weight, aerodynamics and its other fuel-saving features.

The result: a broad spectrum of small, relatively lightweight trailers and motorhomes that were not very roomy inside. Called ultra-lights, they were built with questionable quality, utilizing formerly unacceptable techniques such as hollow-core cabinet doors, foam-core tables and countertops, light-duty axles and suspension systems, marginal framings and thinly laminated sidewalls that literally peeled apart or shook to pieces after the unit had been thoroughly used under real-life travel conditions.

Families that bought those units quite often discovered they had paid more for less.

The trend toward ultra-light RVs did not last long, but the industry learned a great deal during the brief, three-year experimental period before ultra-lights faded from the scene. It learned that, by blending some aspects of the new technology with conventional construction methods, it could produce large, roomy trailers and motorhomes that were not much more expensive than mid-size models. Thus, manufacturers of niche high-end RVs -- such as Holiday Rambler which, in the early 1980s was virtually the only producer of Class A motorhomes longer than 30 feet -- suddenly found themselves sharing the market with literally dozens of competitors that were producing 32 to 36-foot RVs that were priced for entry-level buyers.

BACK-TO-BASICS MOVEMENT

The next stage in the RV industry's evolution was a back-to-basics movement that started early in the 1980s and continued until one company single-handedly changed it during the latter part of the decade. As part of that trend, RV manufacturers theoretically reduced both weight and cost by producing units that were equipped with relatively few standard features. This practice allowed the customer to add whatever options he wanted, often not realizing that he was not only paying a premium price for those options, but also that he was adding weight which, in all likelihood, caused his RV to be too near (or even over) its gross vehicle weight rating.

Thus, in 1985, it was possible to buy a new 33-foot Rainbow Class A motorhome for about $35,000 or a 34-foot Komfort travel trailer for only $16,000. However, neither unit was equipped with the type of features most families wanted and, as options, the cost of those features was quite high -- and many of those RVs were unaffordable. At that time, manufacturers and dealers alike earned phenomenal profits from options: A factory-installed TV antenna or furnace, for example, was marked up about 150% to the dealer, and the dealer added another 75-80%. Thus, an antenna or furnace which cost the manufacturer $10 was sold at wholesale for $25, and the retail customer was charged almost $45. An optional shower enclosure cost the manufacturer $12; it was priced to the dealer at $84 (a 600% markup) and to the retail customer for $168 (an additional 100% markup).

Multi-level profits of that sort were what caused RVs to be priced out of the average family's reach during most of the 1980s.

.The back-to-basics movement led, inevitably, to a whole different marketing and pricing philosophy spearheaded by a small company named Dutchmen. This concept -- which still prevails throughout the industry today -- is based upon the simple idea that an RV manufacturer and its dealers should earn *reasonable* profits from building and selling the RVs themselves, not from relying upon accessories and options sales to produce the profits for them. The result was a strategy of *packaging* RVs with a full range of the features ordered most often by typical retail customers, and the cost of the accessories built into the base price of the RV, not added to it.

THE NEW UPSCALE MODELS

The RV industry's evolution was not yet complete, however. A few builders of entry-level products began a quiet assault on the highly specialized marketplace segments traditionally held by premium companies such as Airstream, Holiday Rambler, Newmar and Carriage. Those companies had, for many years, virtually controlled the high-end and mid-priced towables market segments with their premium-quality trailers that featured aluminum framing, radiused corners, front and rear molded fiberglass caps and a sleek, smooth exterior design.

In a series of low-key maneuvers that turned out to be revolutionary, builders of entry-level RVs began offering unique types of *upscale* travel trailers and fifth-wheels. Priced above entry-level products but below the traditional mid-priced trailers, they fostered a whole new price range of RVs. Like their higher priced competitors, they featured front and rear fiberglass caps and rounded corners for aerodynamics. But instead of being built with aluminum-cage framing, they had frames that were part wood and part aluminum. Their exterior skins, instead of being smooth aluminum, were either smooth or ribbed laminated fiberglass similar to the laminated sidewalls used for several years on Class A motorhomes.

At first, those new trailers were ridiculed by competing dealers and manufacturers because of their so-called *peripheral* aluminum frame sections. But retail buyers liked the trailers; they were sleek, aerodynamic, well equipped and relatively low priced, and they were advertised as having aluminum frames! Equally important, raw wood material prices started skyrocketing, narrowing the historically wide gap between the cost of wood and aluminum. Suddenly, peripheral aluminum framing began to have solid economic appeal.

The result: This new breed of upscale trailers quickly gained the status of respectability. And, as they carved out a solid marketplace niche for themselves, the rest of the RV industry, in its typical bandwagon fashion, rushed to become a part of it. By the spring of 1994, nearly every leading RV manufacturer in America and Canada was producing upscale travel trailers and fifth-wheels built with peripheral aluminum framing. Their price: More than $10,000 under a traditional high-end trailer and $5,000 less than a typical mid-priced coach.

2
SUGGESTED RETAIL PRICES: ARE THEY REAL?

In March 2000, a large RV dealership in Florida circulated an advertisement offering a new 34-foot Flair Class A motorhome for sale. The ad claimed the motorhome's suggested retail value was $92,000, but for a short time, it would be sold at a $15,000 price reduction.

Was that a bargain, or what?

Well, whatever it was, it wasn't a bargain. The *blue book* retail price on that coach was $79,390 -- and that figure was a full 40% markup from its wholesale cost of $57,031. The dealer had assigned his own "suggested retail value" to the motorhome after boosting its price more than 60% above what he'd paid for it. Then, generous businessman that he was, he lowered the price $1,790 under what his every-day window-sticker price should have been and proudly announced he was offering it for sale at a huge discount!

In fact, that motorhome could have been purchased on any day of the year, sale or no sale, for $70,000.

In this case, the dealer's "suggested retail value" was, at best, meaningless and, at worst, a blatant lie.

For many years, RV manufacturers have tried, fruitlessly, to stop their dealers from assigning arbitrary retail prices to their RVs. From the manufacturers' point of view, an RV that is offered for sale at a reasonable price is more likely to sell quickly than one priced above its fair market value. Naturally, more retail sales translate into higher volume for the manufacturers, and most RV companies earn their profits on the basis of volume. By keeping their production lines rolling at peak efficiency and constantly replenishing their dealer networks, they can build their best profits and, at the same time, provide both dealers and retail customers with attractively priced coaches.

Historically, however, dealers have rejected manufacturers' efforts to assign factory-suggested retail prices (SRP) to RVs. Here are their reasons:

•Some dealers insist on pricing the RVs they stock at the highest level they judge the market will accept. They would rather sell a relatively small number of RVs and earn large profits from each one than earn lower profits on a high volume of units. High initial profit and low unit volume also mean fewer financial risks from warranty repairs later.

•Many dealers who handle multiple brands of RVs often use one or more of their brands to *sell against* rather than aggressively trying to sell the units on their own merits. For example, a dealer might stock a few units of Brand A, thereby tying up that brand's franchise so another nearby dealer cannot get it, but he assigns the highest prices possible to each of the Brand A models on his lot. Then he actively promotes the sale of Brand B, a somewhat comparable product that he prices at a lower level. He tells each customer, "Look here. Brand B has exactly the same equipment as Brand A, and it's got a much better price." Thus, his sales of Brand B skyrocket, but sales of Brand A languish.

•A majority of dealers believe the factory has no right to set
suggested retail prices because, they claim, the manufacturer
cannot possibly know the needs of the local marketplace; only
the dealer knows the prices that are appropriate to his locale,
and he should be the one determining the sticker price of each
unit, they maintain.

•Most dealers also believe that factory-suggested retail prices are too low to cover the circumstances in which generous
trade-in allowances are required in order to close a sale. They
claim that either they should have total freedom to determine
retail price or the factory should set its suggested prices at a
higher level than most manufacturers regard as reasonable.
They maintain that a high list price on an RV helps them to
provide generous trade-in allowances to those customers who
believe the RVs they already own are worth more than typical
market value. The dealers say they can always reduce the price
of an RV to whatever figure they wish, and they maintain that
most of the coaches they sell actually cost the customers considerably less than the window-sticker prices.

The debates between dealers and manufacturers over suggested retail prices (SRP) are not likely to be resolved because
the two positions are so far apart on the issue of retail markup.
Most manufacturers would like to see RVs with suggested retail prices that are about 33-35% above wholesale cost; most
dealers insist suggested retail prices should be calculated on
the basis of markups of 40-45%. A few dealers totally reject the
notion of factory-set prices because they believe they should
have the right to sell an RV at a 50-60% markup if they wish
to do so.

Generally speaking, in today's marketplace, most suggested retail prices -- no matter who establishes them -- include dealer markups of between 33 and 40%. But be wary of using that percentage range as a rule of thumb because there are numerous exceptions to it. For example, the manufacturer of a relatively new mini-motorhome recommends that its dealers mark up its coaches only 20%! On the other hand, suggested retail prices for a well known brand of park model trailer include a 45% markup; travel trailers and fifth-wheels bearing an extremely popular brand name are marked up 40%, and a typical folding trailer in today's market is marked up between 33 and 46%, depending upon the policies of its manufacturer and dealers.

To confuse issues even more, one of the best-selling travel trailer brands in America has a suggested retail price that is a phenomenal 47% above its wholesale cost, but the high-end fifth-wheel trailer built by the same company is marked up only 35%! Another major RV producer is quite consistent with its suggested markups: Its full range of folding camping trailers, fifth-wheels, travel trailers and Class C motorhomes are typically marked up 43% by dealers.

The fact is, the only guideline that can be applied to RV retail prices in all cases is this: ***The price assigned to an RV by the selling dealer is the highest amount the dealer believes he can get for the unit within a specific period of time.*** And profit motive aside, an RV's actual selling price is going to be determined by the age-old law of supply and demand.

In this area, dealers have a significant advantage when it comes to negotiating with consumers over price. They know, absolutely, what their current supply-and-demand situation is, and most consumers cannot even guess at it. But any astute shopper who takes into account several important seasonal variances, that, year in and year out, have application in the sales of most recreational vehicles, can still negotiate price quite effectively. These variances include the following:

  ·The competitiveness of the local RV marketplace.

  ·Availability of show or lot "specials."

  ·Availability of manufacturer-sponsored rebates or discounts.

  ·The current popularity of the RV model or floorplan sought.

  ·How a particular model fits into current local or national trends.

  ·How heavily stocked the dealership is with both new and used units.

  ·The time of year as it relates to both seasonal use and the dealer's model-year changeover.

  ·The current aggressiveness of specific RV manufacturers.

  We'll deal with these variances in detail in Chapter 5, but first, let's expand our discussion of advertised or suggested retail prices.

IT'S OPEN TO NEGOTIATION

The suggested retail price of most new RVs is going to be between 33 and 45% above what the dealer paid for it. You also should be aware that in most marketplace circumstances, dealers are quite happy to earn a profit of 30-35%, and that means any more markup than that is open to negotiation, especially if a trade-in is not involved.

As a prospective buyer, your first step, then, should be to learn the *published* suggested retail price of the models that interest you most, and you can do that simply by asking your local dealer to show you the wholesale appraisal guide he uses. There are two national guides published, and virtually every bonafide RV dealership uses one or both of them. Although information in the guides vary somewhat, their published figures are not so far apart that they cannot be used as guidelines. The National Automobile Dealers Association produces an updated national edition of its *NADA Recreational Vehicle Appraisal Guide* three times annually; it lists RVs of all types that were built not only during the current model year, but also for the last 25 years; each unit's new suggested retail price is specified. The other resource is the *Kelley Blue Book Official RV Guide*, which also is updated three times annually; it is published in two versions -- one including towable RVs and the other including motorhomes, pickup campers and van conversions.

If a dealer refuses to show you his wholesale appraisal guide, maybe he is marking up his RVs considerably higher than the industry standards. That does not necessarily mean you should not do business with him, but you should be hesitant to believe what he tells you. Your next step should be to visit a competitor's sales lot and, once again, ask to see an appraisal guide, using it to compare the prices of both dealers' products. If you still cannot get access to one of the guides, stop at the research section of the main library in any sizable city or go directly to the NADA or Kelley Blue Book sites on the Internet.

CALCULATE YOUR OWN PRICE

Once you know a unit's suggested retail price, you should make an assumption -- that the published suggested retail price is approximately 40% higher than the unit's wholesale price. Keep in mind, this assumption might not be entirely correct because, as we've explained, published retail prices for some brands are as low as 33% above their wholesale costs. But it is nearly always safe to use to the 40% figure as a guideline to help you determine what you reasonably ought to expect to pay. So divide the SRP by 1.4 to calculate an estimated whole-sale price; then multiply that figure by 1.30 to determine the retail price of the unit with a 30% markup. Under most circumstances, you should be on firm ground negotiating with the dealer for that price; it will provide the dealer with a reasonable profit under most marketplace circumstances.

If you're a very bold or aggressive shopper, you might even consider asking a few dealers if they will show you their wholesale invoices for the units that interest you. Most dealers will refuse to do that, but some will comply. Otherwise, shop around, seeking comparison prices for specific models. By comparing those prices with the figure you've already determined is reasonable to pay (that is, estimated wholesale price plus 30%), you can get a clearer picture of how accurate your wholesale price estimate was. Be aware, however, that high-volume dealers sometimes are willing to take profits considerably lower than 30% in order to sell certain models quickly.

In today's highly competitive automobile sales environment, many of us know about new car dealerships that are willing to sell their cars at $500 or less over invoice. RV dealerships do not generally operate on that low of a profit margin, but I have my own guidelines for how many dollars most dealers expect to earn from a typical RV sale. And as RV buyers become more sophisticated in their shopping, I expect the day to arrive when dealers will be asked to sell units for a specific dollar-amount above wholesale invoice costs.

Consequently, if I were shopping for a new RV today, I would not hesitate to offer dealers specific dollar-amount profits for their RVs. The chart on the next page is based on my personal evaluation of the profit levels most dealers regard as reasonable during <u>normal</u> business periods. Please keep in mind that competitive and seasonal variances, as well as manufacturer rebates and discounts, can make these guideline profits either low or high. And above a price of about $120,000, it is impossible to predict the amount of profit any dealer will find acceptable. All pricing and markup rules have little or no application for anyone negotiating to buy luxury-class motorhomes.

As an example of how strong competition alone can affect these guidelines, during the summer of 2000, most RV dealers who faced strong competition in their locales seldom earned more than $6,000 to $8,000 gross profit from selling RVs retailing for $50,000 to $150,000. And many of the dealers that stocked luxury-class motorhomes in the $200,000 price range reported they felt fortunate to gross $10,000 from the sale of those units.

Obviously, therefore, an astute buyer who is aware local dealers are facing highly competitive pressures can save himself tens of thousands of dollars by scaling back this guidelines chart dramatically and offering a dealer perhaps half the markup that even I regard as reasonable.

Let's assume, then, that you live in an area which either has been hard hit by an economic downturn or which, for other reasons, has competing RV dealerships that are willing to reduce their prices to the bone. My best advice to you would be to go through the steps of estimating an RV's wholesale cost, then offer to buy the unit for 10% above that figure (or an 8% markup if the suggested retail price is above $65,000). If the dealer rejects your offer -- or laughs at what he regards as a ridiculously low price -- ask him to make you a counter-offer. But be warned: If you offer a low-profit price that the dealer accepts, you should be ready to make the purchase; don't play the unethical game of winning major concessions from the dealer and then shopping elsewhere for an even better deal.

THE REBATE DIFFERENCE

Factory rebates to dealers can have a tremendous impact on dealers' direct-sales profits. Generally speaking, rebates are seldom more than $500-$1,000 for RVs under $30,000; they are typically $2,000-$5,000 for RVs that are retail-priced at $30,000 to $80,000, but they can be as high as $10,000 for luxury-class motorhomes costing $100,000 or more. Factory rebates usually are not well publicized, but the discerning shopper can become aware of them by asking dealers if they're willing to pass on part or all of any rebates.

Typically, when factory rebates are offered to dealers, most dealers are willing to take their profits directly from the rebates and sell the RVs either at or just above their wholesale invoice costs. During the economic downturn of 1990-91, many dealers literally stayed in business by slashing their up-front prices and counting on rebates to support their operations. In most rebate situations, a dealer qualifies for large rebates only when he buys a specified number of units from the factory; therefore, he must in turn retail all or most of those units at whatever price he can in order to make the rebates profitable for himself.

At times, factory rebates are paid directly to the owner of the dealership, not to the dealership itself, and in such cases, sales personnel are sometimes unaware that the rebates are available. Typically, when that type of rebate circumstance exists, sales people must get the owner's approval for every low-profit deal they make. Sometimes, the owner/dealer will not even permit his sales personnel to negotiate with customers who are interested in RVs with rebates on them; he insists upon working directly with the customers himself. Obviously, in those circumstances, it is to the buyer's advantage to negotiate with the owner rather than with a sales person.

Factory discounts also are offered to dealers from time to time, but about the only way a prospective buyer can make those discounts work for him is to ask the dealer to pass on the discounted savings (more about this in Chapter 4). RV manufacturers offer discounts for a variety of reasons, ranging from the need to build a dealer network in a particular locale to the desire to increase plant production levels, and the amount of discounts are quite varied -- from as little as $50 to as much as 15% -- depending upon the manufacturer's marketing strategy.

SHOW SPECIALS

So-called *show specials* are another matter. Such specials are created for a variety of reasons, but most often, they are offered in order to build a dealership's traffic volume, to reduce inventory or to move specific models quickly. Whatever the reason, show special prices usually bear a direct relationship to the amount of profit a dealership tries to earn from the sale of all its units. Therefore, most show specials are merely reductions of 10 or 15% from the day-to-day selling price of the units. A few dealers such as the one mentioned in the beginning of this chapter add extra markup to an RV, creating a false "suggested retail value," and then reduce that price to a level they think will appeal to buyers; this practice is clearly unethical, however, and most dealers do not engage in it.

Keep one important fact in mind about show special prices: *The special price always will be high enough to provide the dealer with negotiating comfort if the buyer expects a large trade-in allowance.* For that reason alone, an astute buyer can usually win even more price concessions if he does not trade in his old RV on the new one.

As a prospective buyer, it probably is not necessary for you to know the reason why a dealer has lowered his price to a "special" level. But you can be sure of one thing: The dealer is ready to sell that unit, and any others like it, as quickly as possible. You can use that knowledge to advantage by asking the dealer for price reductions of 10-30% below the special price.

3
NEW RVS VS. USED ONES

There are times when buying a *used* recreational vehicle makes more sense than investing in a *new* one. But there are just as many good reasons for purchasing a new unit instead of a used one. It's an age-old dilemma that also confounds buyers of automobiles, trucks, boats and houses, and for some of the same reasons. With RVs in particular, however, the dilemma has been given an added dimension in recent years by companies that have found ways to build new RVs that are no more expensive than late-model used ones. Therefore, price -- once the primary motivator that encouraged used RV purchases -- is less of a consideration than it once was.

Rather than considering just price, today's buyer should give equal weight to the RV's value and benefits. When that is done, it is clear that new RVs have some definite advantages, and used units have others.

For example, here are some reasons why it sometimes is easier to buy a new RV than a used one:

•Financing is less difficult to arrange.

•Banks and financial agencies have fewer questions about a new RV's loan value; they do not have to judge its condition in order to determine how much they can loan on it.

•Lower down payments are required for new RVs than for used ones the same price.

•Loan periods often are typically longer for new RVs, permitting the buyer to make smaller monthly payments.

•Virtually all new RVs have strong warranty programs, and many manufacturers offer optional extended warranties at reasonable rates.

•New RVs usually are equipped with more up to date appliances.

•New units usually feature the newest trends in floorplans, fabrics, construction techniques and furnishings.

On the other hand, here are some good reasons for buying a used RV instead of a new one:

•Both insurance and license plate fees are generally more expensive for new RVs than for used ones.

•Used units have far less depreciation than new ones, and because of a new RV's initial depreciation, it is possible to buy a used luxury-class RV for about the same price that a more basically equipped new one costs.

•Since RVs are built for long-term use, a used unit quite likely will see as many years of satisfactory service from a family as a new one.

•A well-built used unit that has a few years of camping behind it is quite likely to be free of irritating little problems that typically plague the owners of new RVs.

Except for fully equipped luxury-class models, new RVs in the past were sold as relatively basic products that needed a wide range of options to make them comfortable for year-around travel. The owners of those rigs paid premium prices to upgrade their refrigerators and furnaces and to add awnings, larger LP-gas bottles, air conditioners, generators and microwave ovens. All that has changed during recent years with the new trend toward factory packaging; even the lowest priced RVs of 2001 frequently roll out of the factories with a full selection of features, and those units are priced to compete directly against late-model used RVs.

As a result, during the spring of 2001, the suggested retail price of a new 31-foot Dutchmen front-kitchen travel trailer was $17,663, while a five-year-old 1996 Aluma-Lite travel trailer the same size retailed for $17,559. Which coach was the better buy? There's no question the Aluma-Lite was a better-built trailer when it was new; it featured aluminum cage framing, fiberglass front and rear end caps and better grades of fabric, cabinets and carpeting. But the two trailers were equipped with virtually the same appliances as well as similar tires, brakes, wheels and other features.

Conventional wisdom says that as those trailers age, the new low-end Dutchmen will depreciate faster than the used Alum-Lite. But that ain't necessarily so! Significantly, based on past marketplace performance, in three years today's new Dutchmen will be worth about $10,000, and the eight-year-old Aluma-Lite will cost about $8,500. So which unit has the better value? Your guess is as good as ours.

A more important question that needs answering is: Which trailer will provide its owner with the best performance and satisfaction during the intervening three years?

First-time purchasers of both new and used RVs consistently make two major mistakes when they buy a unit: They select the wrong floorplans, and they choose models that are too small for their needs. Because of those errors, most families trade their first RVs within two or three years; their second units are larger and have floorplans that more closely fit their RVing lifestyles.

Perhaps it's my natural journalistic pessimism, but I'm convinced first-time RV buyers will continue to make those same mistakes no matter how much advice they're given about the importance of making sure the units they buy match their needs and their traveling habits. Therefore, it seems to me that most new camping families should reduce their economic risk and the amount of their first-year depreciation by purchasing used units first instead of new ones.

However, the simple exercise of buying a used recreational vehicle is fraught with hazards.

Most prospective buyers are astute enough to examine a used RV carefully for evidence of leaks, poor workmanship and abuse, but there are other hidden shortcomings which are not quite so evident. For example, thousands of new and almost-new travel trailers and fifth-wheels were shipped to south Florida late in 1992 and used as temporary housing for victims of Hurricane Andrew. Those trailers were badly used and abused -- in effect, subjected to hard every-day living that one expert estimated was equal to ten years of campground use. Throughout the 1990s, trailers used by hurricane victims found their way into the used-RV marketplace, and because Florida was not able to absorb that many used units, thousands of them were wholesaled around the country to RV dealers looking for bargain buys. If you are a prospective purchaser of a used trailer, be certain you don't buy one of those units or, if you do buy one, make the purchase with a full awareness of what you're getting.

Hundreds of other RVs were sold throughout the Midwest that were seriously damaged during the floods of 1993 and 1995. Many of those were reconditioned and fitted with new furniture and replacement appliances. But flood-damaged RVs should be avoided; the water damage inside walls, in the roof and under the floor can never truly be repaired, and silt residue can cause other serious problems in appliances such as water heaters, furnaces, ranges and refrigerators.

LEARN ABOUT ITS HISTORY

Learning about potential structural damage is an excellent reason for talking with the current or previous owner before committing yourself to buy a used RV. If you are considering buying from a private individual, question him thoroughly about how his family used the unit and ask him point-blank about its shortcomings. Remember that the perfect recreational vehicle has not yet been built, and I've *never* seen an RV that lacked problems. If you're buying from an RV dealer, ask for the name and address of the previous owner, and then call that person and discuss the unit's history. Learn as much as you can about serious problem areas:

•Did it ever have roof leaks or window leaks? If so, how and when were they repaired? Who did the work, and was it done satisfactorily?

•How much and what type of insulation is in the RV? Don't be swayed by R-factors someone quotes to you; in most RVs, they are relatively meaningless. Did the previous owner experience any cold-weather problems, such as drafts or condensation, in the unit?

•Was the unit ever wrecked? If so, who repaired it?

•Were any problems ever experienced with the refrigerator, range, oven, furnace, air conditioner, toilet, propane system, awning, sewage system, water heater?

•How was the RV used? On long trips, short trips, weekends? How many people camped in it? Did family members complain about problems with seating, sleeping space or storage space?

•How was periodic maintenance such as leak protection and winterizing handled?

•Was there ever any problem with electrical polarity?

Don't underestimate the seriousness of water leaks; they are the worst enemy of an RV's structure. Water that seeps into the roof and sidewalls is absorbed by insulation and, over a period of time, it reacts chemically with plywood, glue, metal and other structural components to cause major problems. Water can literally cause an RV to come apart from the inside out!

DON'T BUY A DINOSAUR

Another danger in buying a used RV is that you might be convinced to purchase a dinosaur -- that is, an RV that has serious resale limitations because there is something inherently wrong with it that might not be obvious to the inexperienced buyer. An example of a dinosaur is a late-model fifth-wheel with a double-slideout floorplan. Although slideouts have become immensely popular, there are virtually no new fifth-wheels being built any longer with two small slideouts -- typically, one in the living area that contains a sofa and one in the kitchen that contains a dinette. Since 1992, the industry-wide trend in fifth-wheels has been toward floorplans with large 13- to 18-foot slideout sections that contain both the sofa and dinette as well as other special features. The RV marketplace switched from double-slideout models to large-slideout models so quickly that many dealers were caught with double-slide units on the lots, unsold. Although those trailers will be offered for sale at bargain prices for several years, they do not sell quickly, and their future trade-in value is very poor.

Another type of dinosaur is a Class A motorhome with a rear bathroom. Popular for a relatively brief period during the early 1980s, that floorplan faded into obscurity because campers discovered they did not like the lack of privacy that was necessitated when their bedroom was near mid-coach, just forward of the bathroom. Although the arrangement permitted the motorhome to be equipped with a phenomenally large bathroom, that benefit did not outweigh the lack-of-privacy disadvantage.

One irony of RV design is that custom-built or one-of-a-kind floorplans can be virtually impossible to resell. A snowbirding couple we know had all their cabinettops built about four inches lower than usual in their custom trailer because the wife was quite short. When it came time for them to upgrade to a new trailer, no one wanted their old one. Similarly, our family came up with what we thought was an excellent interior design for a motorhome: We had ours built with two facing sofa-beds that met in the center of the coach, forming one huge bed at night. Plus, it provided two excellent lounging spots at night for either reading or watching TV. But apparently, other RVers didn't like the design as well as we did; potential buyers stood in line NOT to purchase it at trade-in time!

WATCH OUT FOR CON ARTISTS

Buyers of used RVs also should be careful not to be victimized by members of two ethnic clans of con artists that sell nearly new travel trailers from street corners, campground sites and motel parking lots. Of Irish and Scottish descent, these clans -- who call themselves Travelers -- buy cheap trailers from three Indiana factories and resell them immediately after telling their victims hard-luck stories about personal misfortunes that are forcing them to sell their beautiful new RVs. The trailers have relatively worthless warranties because they must be returned to the factory for repairs, and most RV dealers refuse to service them. The Irish and Scottish Travelers -- referred to as "gypsies" throughout the RV industry -- actually live full-time in the trailers while they travel around the country engaging in a wide variety of fraudulent business practices.

Generally speaking, the trailers will be offered for sale by young and middle-aged women who are either living in the coaches or are registered at nearby economy-priced motels. The women will be polite, well dressed and outgoing. They will tell sad stories about family illnesses or other personal tragedies that are wholly fictional but are calculated to provoke sympathy.

While the women stay "home" and sell trailers, their husbands and sons are scouring residential areas in search of other victims for their various home remodeling scams: roof sealing, driveway paving or sealing, house painting, tree trimming, lawn care, chimney repair, lightning rod installation. And, during their short-term stops in various communities, most of the family members -- including the children -- will participate in major shoplifting expeditions to department stores, a wide range of insurance fraud schemes, and a series of con games such as fake charitable solicitations, so-called *pigeon drops* and sleight-of-hand currency transactions at banks and other businesses.

Although the Travelers originally built their reputation as itinerant horse traders, during the last 30 years they have relied on flashy pickup trucks towing travel trailers to provide them both with mobile living quarters and an extra means of earning cash. Typically, they buy their trailers from the Elkhart factories for about $9,000-$16,000 each and then resell them for $14,000 to $24,000.

The trailers carry a wide range of familiar sounding but obscure brand names which are changed frequently. Only one of the three manufacturers has a dealer network of any kind, and that one's list of dealerships is quite small -- and confidential!

The Travelers tend to prey on inexperienced first-time RV buyers who are unfamiliar with popular brand names, but thousands of experienced campers also have been duped by the slick-talking con artists. They are so skillful at selling trailers from campgrounds that a single family has been known to move as many as a dozen coaches from the same campsite during a two-week period. As soon as one trailer is sold, a family member drives quickly to Elkhart for another, and it is commonplace for Travelers to live in and sell as many as three or four coaches at the same time, constantly replacing sold units with new ones.

Ironically, even though the Travelers live on the fringe of society in a low-profile underground criminal network, they are easy to spot.

Nearly always, their trailers will be parked together at campgrounds in two to six adjoining campsites. They tow their trailers with expensive, fully equipped pickup trucks that are always kept sparkling clean. Parked along with the trailers will be one or more distinctive other vehicles: a driveway paving truck (usually red) that might be towing a flatbed trailer holding a small motorized blacktop roller; one or more trucks containing large tanks of driveway/roof sealing compound, and perhaps an expensive fully enclosed utility trailer. Most Traveler families also own two or three new automobiles, and those range from sporty Pontiac Firebirds to Lincoln Town Cars.

The utility trailers are used for carrying family clothing and other personal possessions, although sometimes they also contain carpets, linoleum, jewelry and mass-produced consumer items that the families sell in their various scams.

Strangely, Travelers prefer to buy and sell travel trailers with a unique, easily identifiable feature -- an entryway with sliding glass patio-type doors instead of a standard entry door. Few, if any, bonafide travel trailer manufacturers have built coaches with that type of entry since the late 1970s, but the Travelers regard the sliding glass door as beautiful and functional. Over the years, the manufacturers supplying trailers to the Travelers also have focused heavily upon building units with outdated "tip-out" room extensions -- a type of feature that virtually no other RV builder still provides. Lately, however, two of the three companies have started offering travel trailers (and now fifth-wheels) with more up to date slideout extensions.

The three Elkhart manufacturers -- which we cannot identify here for legal reasons -- have such a low profile within the RV industry that most industry leaders have never even heard of them. But all three are so successful that they consistently rank among the top twenty travel trailer producers in the nation in terms of unit retail sales! Through the Travelers, they each sell more travel trailers annually than 80% of America's other RV companies.

At the same time, two of the three companies have so routinely ignored and violated the RV industry's venting and plumbing standards that the personal safety of anyone who buys their products must be questioned.

How can you and your friends avoid being the victims of the traveling con artists? Here are our recommendations:

•First, make certain that any RV you buy is being sold by a person who is firmly entrenched in the community and is not just passing through. Although doing this should prevent you from buying an RV from a Traveler, it is not altogether foolproof; segments of the Travelers have established permanent residences near Fort Worth, Memphis, Orlando and Augusta, Georgia, and occasionally sell trailers from their homes.

•Second, ask a local RV dealer to tell you the names of so-called "gypsy" trailers that he is aware are being sold within the community. Then simply stay away from those brands.

•Third, do not fall for sad stories about family emergencies, broken marriages or engagements, unexpected deaths or financial crises.

•Fourth, watch for the distinctive features mentioned earlier -- sliding glass patio doors, outdated tip-out room extensions and the presence of driveway sealing/paving equipment.

In case you are tempted to buy a Traveler's trailer (and many consumers do it knowing full well are buying inferior coaches), keep in mind that the Travelers are stopped in your community for one primary reason: so that they can practice their wide range of frauds on your neighbors. They do not

spend time in communities where they cannot earn several
thousand dollars a week through con games, shoplifting and
insurance fraud.

4
HOW TO FIND BARGAINS

Bargain prices on RVs are available nearly all the time for someone who knows where and how to find them, but a shrewd shopper who is able to make his purchase when the bargains are most plentiful can literally save thousands of dollars.

On the following pages, I'll tell you the secrets of finding bargains that no one else knows are available. First, though, let's look at the types of bargains that are available to everyone.

Under normal circumstances, and in normal market conditions, *the best time to buy a new or used RV is in the off-season* -- preferably, between September and December in most parts of the country (even in sunbelt states). A private seller typically wants to dump his RV before he has to store it for winter, and an RV dealer wants to trim his interest expense, increase his cash flow and reduce his off-season lot inventory to make room for next season's new models and trade-ins. Absolutely the best time to buy an RV from a dealer is two days after cold weather and a heavy snowfall have resulted in a discouraging low amount of buyer traffic at the dealership. Frequently, good deals on used RVs also can be found at dealerships between January and March because sales of used units during that period can help a dealer's cash flow and allow him to build a larger inventory of new RVs.

Model and floorplan selections are often quite limited, however, during the late fall and early winter months when bargains are easiest to find. Conversely, the best time to shop for floorplans and models is February through May and, although that period is not always the best time to find bargains, some are available due to pre-season sales and travel show specials.

The worst time to buy any RV is just before you're ready to leave on an RV trip! I once helped my son sell his trailer to a family that mentioned they were scheduled to begin a camping trip to Disney World within a week. It was clear to me that they did not have much time to buy an RV for their vacation; the pressure was on them to buy, not on me to sell. Other times when you're less likely to negotiate the best possible price are in late spring and early summer when demand for new and used RV is at its highest.

Public RV shows and dealer lot promotions are rather good times to buy RVs -- even used ones, although used units are not typically displayed at the shows or offered at special prices on the lots. At such times, though, dealership personnel are mentally geared to sell as much as they can, and they are usually willing to make show special prices available to shoppers astute enough to ask for them.

THE BEST BARGAINS

During normal business periods, the best bargains are usually found in specific types of RVs:

•Travel trailers of 26-29 feet with front kitchens.

•Fifth-wheels 28-30 feet with large slideouts, especially rear-kitchen models.

•Mini-motorhomes 27-29 feet long with rear queen-size beds and L-shaped mid-coach galleys.

•Eight-foot folding camping trailers.

•Soft-side pop-up pickup campers and larger high-end campers that are basically substitutes for mini-motorhomes.

•Economy-priced Class A motorhomes 28-30 feet long.

•Entry-level camping vans.

Bargains are normally difficult to find among custom-built RVs, ultra-luxurious Class A motorhomes, high-end folding camping trailers and luxury-class fifth-wheels and travel trailers.

GLUT OF USED TRAILERS

Bargain-priced used RVs were quite easy to find throughout the 1990s in the eastern half of the U.S. due almost entirely to the glut of units that were temporarily occupied in Florida by victims of 1992's Hurricane Andrew. Thousands of those hard-used RVs were poured into the marketplace during 1993 and 1994 after the victims found permanent housing, and they caused prices of most used RVs to plunge. Those bargains did not include high-end products of any type, however, because RVs in the upper price range were not generally utilized by hurricane victims. The same glut of used units adversely affected trade-in allowances in the Midwest, South and Southeast.

When they can be found, some of the best bargains are new trailers and motorhomes that are a couple of years old. As those never-sold units age and add birthdays, their prices will continue to decline, and a shopper who is not too picky about floorplan or furnishings could even find occasional mid-priced motorhomes and trailers priced below what the dealers originally paid for them!

One of the best examples of that was told to me in early June 2001 by a woman who bought a new $250,000 Mountain Aire Class A motorhome for only $155,000. The 40-foot coach was a 2000-model that had already spent its first birthday sitting, unwanted, on a dealer's lot, and it was literally weeks away from its second birthday. The lady said it had a "putrid" maroon decor, and it had been moved from one dealership to another in hopes a retail buyer could be found.

Although the woman didn't know the history of the motorhome, my investigation revealed it had been stocked originally by a dealer who thought he had a buyer for it but was unable to sell it because of its decor. The company then moved the coach to its top dealership in Elkhart, Indiana, in hope of finding a buyer for it. The lady and her husband decided to purchase it because of its extremely low price and because they were willing to spend a few thousand dollars to change the interior colors.

Early 2001 turned out to be the best period for finding bargains in Class A motorhomes that I've seen for many years. In fact, motorhome bargains were quite plentiful through most of 2000, and as this is written in June 2001, I expect excellent bargains in those coaches to be available at least through the end of the year and probably into 2002!

The widespread *buyer's market* existed due to a series of unusual circumstances. First, the nation's economy had been quite good for several years; gasoline prices were low, and RV sales were booming. Those conditions, along with aggressive incentive programs by RV manufacturers, prompted dealers around the country to stock their lots heavily with big, expensive Class A's.

Then, to everyone's surprise, gasoline prices skyrocketed in mid-2000 at the same time the nation's economy stopped growing. High gasoline prices, coupled with worries about inflation and a series of declines in the stock market (particularly technical stocks), caused RV-buying consumers to become more cautious about their purchases, and retail sales of RVs -- but particularly the already-overstocked Class A's -- declined sharply. Dealerships around the country found themselves burdened with far too many luxury-class motorhomes on which they were paying their lending institutions interest.

The Class A market floundered through the 2000 model year and the winter of 2000-01, with dealers hoping for lower gasoline prices when the weather warmed. Instead, gasoline prices continued to climb and reached more than $2 per gallon in some sections of the country. By the time the spring of 2001 arrived, dealers were scrambling to unload their excess inventory, cut their interest payments and make room for smaller, less expensive RVs.

Bargains weren't available in just Class A motorhomes, either. In New England, dealers were overstocked with folding camping trailers and small, lightweight travel trailers and fifth-wheels. In Snowbird country -- south Texas, Florida, southern California and Arizona -- large towables and diesel pusher Class A's were being discounted heavily. Virtually everywhere, mid-size and large travel trailers were available at bargain prices. And, as spring moved toward summer and the 2002 model year loomed, those never-sold 2000 and 2001 models (and even some 1999s!) were offered nation-wide as bargains not seen since the early 1990s.

As always, retail prices of current models decline the closer we get to a new model-year introduction date. *Some of the year's best bargains will always be available in July during year-end clearances.*

OFF-SEASON FOLDING TRAILERS

Folding camping trailers are, as most people in the RV industry will admit, a rather peculiar type of recreational vehicle. The marketing rules and strategies that apply to most other RVs often do not apply to them. And, not coincidentally, folding trailers can be purchased every year at bargain prices due to one of the unique ways they are marketed.

Each fall, virtually all folding trailer manufacturers offer huge discounts to dealers as part of their annual *winter stocking* program. That program is designed to keep manufacturers' production schedules relatively high during winter months when folding trailers sell poorly. From a dealer's point of view, he can purchase truckloads of folding trailers at prices that are not available to him any other time and then, when spring arrives, he will be ready for buyers with a good inventory of units. Retail customers who are aware of a dealership's participation in winter stocking programs can nearly always negotiate purchasing a new folding trailer at a bargain price. For the dealer, a few folding trailers sold during the winter at prices just above his cost just means fewer units that he has to hold on his lot until spring.

Often, winter stocking programs are blended with attractive manufacturer-sponsored trips and interest-free stocking incentives so that sometimes, dealers can reap valuable rewards even if they sell a few folding trailers at or below their own invoice costs! Clearly, the family which wants to buy a folding camping trailer should seriously consider making the purchase during the middle of winter. Even if the fold-out has to be stored for several months before it is used, the savings that are available are worth it.

SAVING TRANSPORTATION CHARGES

One final warning about bargains that are available under normal circumstances: Many people believe they can save a substantial amount of money by purchasing an RV directly from the manufacturer or from a dealership near the factory. First of all, except for a few small companies that specialize in customer-direct sales and custom-built units (see Chapter 8), there are no RV manufacturers that sell directly to retail customers. Consider that concept for a moment: Why would an RV manufacturer risk alienating its dealer network by selling a few units from time to time, at discount prices, to its dealers' prospects?

On the other hand, many RV manufacturers are quite willing to work closely with the retail customer who is actually buying a coach through his local dealer. And some RV companies even allow the retail customer to save delivery charges by picking up his new RV at the plant rather than at the dealership (most manufacturers do levy pick-up or preparation charges for factory deliveries, however). Freight charges from an RV plant to a dealership range from a low of 65 cents to approximately $1.50 per mile, depending upon the type of RV and a manufacturer's wholesale freight policies, so customer pickup at a plant can, indeed, result in substantial savings. Note: Those delivery rates can vary widely with the fluctuation of gasoline prices; obviously, when gasoline is $2 per gallon, delivery charges are going to be higher than when gas is only $1.15 per gallon.

The fact is, transportation charges often (but not always) can be saved when an RV is purchased from a dealership that is located close to the factory. Realizing that, thousands of families drive to Elkhart, Indiana, each year so they can purchase new RVs a few miles from the factories where they are built.

There are two factors those families ought to consider when shopping for bargains in that manner, however. The first is that more and more RV manufacturers are implementing flat-rate freight programs. That means every dealership within the manufacturer's network pays the same amount for freight regardless of the dealership's location. This type of program eliminates the competitive edge that a dealership located near the factory has over more distantly located dealerships simply because of low freight charges.

Secondly, the retail buyer should consider how and where he will get his new unit serviced after he buys it. Unless he intends to take it back to the dealership where he bought it every time it needs work done on it, he will have to find a dealership near his home to provide that service. In theory, every dealership is obliged to perform service for the owners of each brand the dealership handles, no matter where the unit was purchased. But in reality, dealerships have little sympathy for local residents who buy their rigs elsewhere; they usually won't refuse to service such a unit, but they will insist upon helping their own customers first. Therefore, I always recommend that shoppers consider the alternatives very seriously before they decide not to buy their new RVs from local dealers.

From time to time, unusual marketplace conditions come together to create what can only be described as a buyer's market for RV purchases. These periods are usually -- but not always -- related either to a national economic downturn such as a recession or to exceptionally high gasoline prices such as those of 2000-01. The marketplace is affected most severely when gasoline availability is questionable, but we have not experienced a period such as that since the early 1980s. At times, the downturn may be only regional or state-wide in its scope. But however widespread it is, it will have a profound affect on at least some segments of the RV industry.

Keep in mind this fact: The RV industry *ALWAYS* leads the national or regional economy both into and out of a recession. Furthermore, the companies that produce high-end RV products always lead the *INDUSTRY* in those directions.

To illustrate this, let's look at the products built by one company -- Airstream. Typically, a few months before the rest of the industry notices a slowing trend leading toward a recession, sales of Airstream travel trailers will begin to falter; similarly, Airstream sales traditionally improve several months before those of other brands as a national economic recession bottoms out. During the slowing trend, bargains for dealer-stocked models will be easy to find; conversely, not many Airstream bargains will be available when sales of the brand improve dramatically following a recession; for a time during the initial regrowth period, both new and used Airstream trailers might even be hard to find at any price until the company's production schedule is at full steam and its dealers' inventories are replenished.

LOWER DEALER INVENTORIES

During a local or national economic downturn, RV dealer inventories will almost always be reduced dramatically -- purposely so, because the dealers do not want to pay interest on products they are unable to sell, and they want to have lot space open so that when the economy improves, they will be prepared to restock with the latest models. During such periods, bargains are difficult, but not impossible, to find. The best bargains at such times are for units with unusual or rather specialized floorplans and for models that have been discontinued by manufacturers. Usually, those RVs are mid-priced or high-end products, but they often can be purchased at near (or even below) their wholesale invoice prices simply because the dealer wants to stop paying interest on them and open lot space for models that help his cash flow.

During slow periods, some RV manufacturers even encourage their dealers to sell stocked models at bargain prices. They do that by, in effect, subsidizing the sale of inventoried units; they offer dealers either a discount or purchase credits each time a product already at the dealership is sold and immediately replaced by a new coach. This type of arrangement can have a snowballing effect on a dealer's sales: By selling a new unit from his lot that may be the previous year's model, he gets a more up to date model (at a bargain price) to replace it, and the moment he sells that replacement unit, he gets another discount or credit on the next replacement unit, and so on. Buyers can nearly always take advantage of this unusual marketing practice because it is to the dealer's benefit, for cash-flow reasons, to move each new model off his lot as quickly as possible, and so he offers the units at prices that will enable him to sell them fast. The arrangement all[...] [op]portunity to build sales volume even dur[ing...] [con]ditions, and for consumers, it is a chance to buy a[...] extraordinarily low price.

As in the case with other dealer sales incentive programs such as discounts and rebates, the retail shopper often has to learn from dealers which manufacturer programs are available so that he can take advantage of them. For that reason alone, one of the first questions a shopper should ask a dealer is what kind of incentive programs are currently being offered by the dealer's RV suppliers.

Following the end of high gasoline prices or national recessionary periods, and even slow economic periods within specific regions of the country, RV manufacturers will always be faced with rebuilding their dealer networks and restocking their existing dealerships. One way they will do that is by offering *NEW* dealers special stocking incentives and, at the same time, making it easier for their existing dealerships to rebuild inventories. For example, during the months following the 1991-92 economic downturn, most manufacturers refrained from increasing their wholesale prices, even though their own costs increased, and many RV companies even lowered their prices in order to encourage their dealers to restock merchandise. I expect the same reluctance to raise prices when currently high gasoline prices return to normal; RV manufacturers and their dealers will be more concerned about building sales volume than in making profits from individual unit sales.

Even though manufacturers could theoretically find them-ves in legal hot water if they offered newly recruited dealerships special price breaks for taking on their lines, there are ways around that, and most manufacturers are bold and aggressive enough following a recession to do whatever it takes to expand their dealer networks. For that reason, shoppers should always be alert for the sudden appearance of a new RV brand at a local dealership; although arrival of that new brand might simply mean that the dealership is expanding and adding more lines because business is so good, it also could signal that the dealer has been provided with special price breaks by the manufacturer of that brand, and chances are good that at least some models of the new brand will be sold at reduced prices.

One popular angle used by manufacturers to recruit new dealerships is to offer interest-free stocking on the dealers' initial orders. For the dealer adding an expensive line of RVs, a 90-day interest-free period can mean thousands of dollars in savings for him. Of course, that arrangement also has the effect of encouraging him to sell those new products as quickly as possible before he has to start paying interest on them. Sometimes, a manufacturer will even allow a new dealer to extend the interest-free offer another 90 days with a *SECOND* stocking or re-stocking.

In any case, it is nearly always to a shopper's advantage to consider an RV brand that is newly offered by a dealership. Both the dealer and the brand's manufacturer will be anxious to prove to each other, and to themselves, that their new business relationship is destined to be successful, so the new products are likely to be priced to sell quickly. A dealership which can prove to its new RV supplier that it is able to turn a high volume of product quickly becomes a favored customer of the manufacturer, and the dealership will receive special favors that are not available to other retailers. In effect, the retail customer who buys a newly stocked brand -- at any price -- from a local dealership is doing that dealership a service!

AVOIDING PRICE INCREASES

But don't forget another aspect of this post-recession recovery period: *RVs that are sold to dealers at recessionary prices are bargains too.* If a manufacturer delays a needed 10% price increase in order to help its dealers restock product, that means buyers can save $1,500 on a $15,000 RV simply by purchasing it *BEFORE* the price increases are implemented.

How can you know when price increases will take effect? Usually, you can't -- because most manufacturers don't tell even their dealers (or their own in-house salesmen, for that matter) about price changes until just a few weeks before the increases are implemented. Generally speaking, however, manufacturers raise their prices only during two periods -- most often at the point of model changeover, and at other times just following the national RV trade show in Louisville, Kentucky (always scheduled the first week after Thanksgiving).

Dealers are informed about price increases just enough in advance so they can clear their lots of old units and replace them with new ones just before the price increases go into effect. A typical practice of manufacturers exhibiting at the Louisville show is to offer dealers an opportunity to order a large volume of units during the show at either lower or pre-increase prices. Since those ordered units do not have to be paid for until they are delivered to the dealerships six to ten weeks later, the dealers are, in effect, buying their spring merchandise at prices lower than they would have to pay if they waited for another month or two to place their orders. Most manufacturers also allow their dealers to take delivery of show-special units over a period of several months, so that some units ordered in December might not reach the dealership until April or May. That policy not only helps the dealership level out its cash flow, but it also enables the manufacturer to keep production at a smooth, efficient pace.

Most dealers are quite willing to tell their customers whenever they make a special buy on new models, and the dealers don't hesitate to give purchasers price breaks on those models. But generally speaking, a shopper has to be astute enough to ask about the dealer's seasonal discount buys in order to learn of them; those purchases are difficult -- and expensive -- for a small dealer to publicize through advertising. Dealerships that order new units in December for delayed delivery also are willing to tell their customers about models that have not yet appeared on their lots, and often, they are happy to negotiate special prices for those units. But you should be aware that the ordered units probably were bought equipped in a specific way, and for delivery at a specific time, and changing an order either for earlier delivery or to add optional equipment might not be possible.

Immediately following exceptionally high gasoline prices or a national economic downturn, some regions of the country will recover slower than others. For example, after the 1991-92 downturn, improved RV sales were experienced throughout the nation except in California and the Northeast, which were slow to recover economically. Similarly, during early 2001 when gasoline prices appeared ready to decline slightly, dealerships in the Midwest were not as heavily overstocked with inventory as dealers in southern California and Arizona, and therefore price discounting was not quite so aggressive there.

Although bargains often can be found within slowly recovering areas following a recovery, RV model and floorplan selection usually is quite poor because dealerships are then usually under-stocked with merchandise -- exactly opposite the situation they faced several months earlier! One key to shopping those areas is being ready to buy just as the economy starts to improve and dealers begin restocking their lots, prompted by manufacturer discounts and other incentives. Sometimes RV companies boost their prices regionally, and when they do that, areas that experience dramatic economic growth often will have fewer bargains available than the regions or states which still have not recovered.

Following a recovery -- or a dramatic growth in sales for a particular type of RV product -- *retail demand often outstrips supply, resulting in higher prices.* Then, with those higher prices frequently comes a slackening of sales, so discounts and incentives are offered in order to recharge retail sales. This type of activity is so poorly planned and implemented, however, that consumers -- and even dealers -- are usually unprepared for a new series of price reductions, so sales tend to stagnate. A perfect illustration of this occurred in 1993-94 following the last economic downturn. Just after the nation's economic condition bottomed, sales of folding camping trailers rebounded suddenly, unexpectedly. Demand immediately exceeded supply, resulting in price increases. With those increases came a decline in the rate of sales growth, followed by another round of price reductions.

Although widespread dealer restockings after a recession historically results in a series of wholesale price increases by RV manufacturers, that scenario did not develop for the full range of RV products after the 1991-92 downturn. Economic recovery was very spotty at first, and key sales states such as Texas, California, Florida and Michigan did not bounce back from the recession quickly. Each of those states is critical for the long-term health of nearly every RV manufacturer, and competition for dealers in the four states continued to be quite intense for two years after the recovery started. Any manufacturer implementing price increases during that period assumed a serious competitive handicap.

On the other hand, as soon as RV sales growth appeared to be solid in New England, the Northwest, most of the South and Midwest and along the Atlantic seaboard, manufacturers started considering ways to increase prices.

COMPETITION BREEDS BARGAINS

It should be no surprise to anyone that bargains are nearly always easier to find in highly competitive environments than they are in areas where a single dealership dominates the marketplace. Cities or states with numerous dealerships consistently have the best competitive atmosphere. Areas hit especially hard by economic downturns usually have fewer dealerships when recoveries begin, and not only are prices likely to be higher due to lack of competition, but some brands and models might not be readily available.

The competitive attitudes of individual dealers also is an

important factor for any bargain-hunter. Those dealers are easy for anyone familiar with the RV industry to identify. They are the dealers who always advertise heavily and offer at least some of their products at significantly reduced prices on a consistent basis. They participate in all the regional RV shows, and they usually set up their own on-location exhibits, complete with food and entertainment, in order to attract potential buyers. They are the real movers and shakers in the RV retail field and can be found nearly everywhere in the country -- in Orlando, Florida; Huntsville, Alabama; Mesa, Arizona; Tampa, Florida; North Little Rock, Arkansas; Greenwood, Indiana; Webster City, Iowa; Mayfield, Kentucky; Thurmont, Maryland; Carthage, Missouri; Colbert, Oklahoma; Junction City, Oregon; Alcoa, Tennessee, and Akron, Ohio.

Another rather consistent pattern related to the economy is this: *During slow sales periods, dealers tend to clear their lots of discontinued brands and slow-moving models, and they tend not to replace those when the economy improves.* Instead, they focus their marketing efforts on models they are certain will sell quickly. As a result, shortages can develop quite easily on models such as mid-priced travel trailers with front living rooms, high-end fifth-wheels for full-time living, mid-priced Class A motorhomes and small 22 to 23-foot Class C motor-homes. Once lot inventories are depleted with those models, the only bargains available for a short time are likely to be for economy-priced RVs with the most popular floorplans. With this scenario comes an out-of-proportion emphasis on entry-level 29-foot travel trailers with front kitchens and both longer and shorter trailers with front bedrooms.

BATCHES AND PACKAGES

About this time, another phenomenon will develop and become widespread: Manufacturers will try to increase their production levels and, at the same time, improve their market shares. Most of them will do that by offering dealers some version of a high-volume purchasing program. The most popular of those programs is one in which the dealers order *"batches"* of so-called *"standard-run"* models. That is, the dealers are given opportunity to buy quantities of a popular RV model, length and floorplan equipped at the factory exactly the way most typical customers buy it. Ordered in "batches" of six, eight or twelve units at a time, those RVs are sold to dealers at lower-than-normal prices.

Consumers can take advantage of standard-run purchases by asking that the price breaks be passed on to them in the form of lower prices. Evidence that a dealer is buying RVs on a standard-run basis usually is indicated by the types of RVs he has on his lot. If the inventory includes half a dozen or more models exactly alike except for interior fabric colors or a few other minor variances, chances are good that he is batch-buying at a discount. Keep in mind that dealers try to sell those units quickly so they can restock while the standard-run program is still available to them, and they'll nearly always pass on at least part of their savings to their customers, creating bargains that are not usually seen during expanding market conditions. Those bargains are likely to be available only for a short time, however, and when the incentives are no longer offered, shoppers can expect the bargains to disappear for an entire season.

In a similar manner, dealers are quite often offered special prices on *"packaged"* RVs equipped with factory-installed accessories that are ordinarily extra-cost options but, for a short time, are made available to dealers at either no cost or a relatively low cost. From a manufacturer's point of view, the purpose of option give-aways is to build RV sales volume without offering discounts on the RVs themselves. Usually, the factories offer programs of that type to dealers after making special arrangements with one or more accessory suppliers to provide a high volume of products at a low per-item cost. For example, a trailer producer might receive a price discount from an awning manufacturer in exchange for buying 200 or more awnings during a 30-day off-season period. Or, an awning company might offer a manufacturer a substantial discount on a specific model as an incentive for the manufacturer to switch awning brands. By passing on those savings to its dealers and convincing them to buy more trailers, the manufacturer can increase its RV production and, in theory, earn more profit due to the boost in sales volume.

The direct benefit to consumers is not exactly a lower priced RV, but one that has more extra features for the same price as a base unit.

Special deals on factory-installed awnings, air conditioners, microwave ovens, generators, TV antennas and other high-priced options are advertised with a wide variety of RV brands from time to time. Watch for them because they can represent significant savings.

INNOVATIVE IMITATION

Another method major RV producers use, sometimes quite successfully, to increase their market penetration during slow periods is to innovate their way out of an economic slump. Just before a downturn ends, or as a downturn appear to be looming just ahead, key manufacturers such as Fleetwood, Coachmen, Jayco and Winnebago will introduce new, innovative mo-dels in an attempt to attract buyers who might not otherwise purchase their products. In recent years, Coachmen earned a significant marketplace advantage over its competitors when it unveiled a broad series of mid-priced wide-body RVs with innovative floorplans; Newmar literally created a whole new market niche for itself by offering the first production-line Class A motorhomes with slideouts; and Winnebago surprised everyone in 1993 when it introduced its no-frills, economy-priced Warrior and Passage motorhomes and then followed those a year later with a new small, all-purpose motorhome built jointly with Volkswagen.

Successful innovative products do not always translate directly into bargains for shoppers, but success does breed imitation, and nearly always, the imitations are sold at bargain prices when they are introduced. Following Coachmen's unexpected success with its new wide-body products, nearly every important manufacturer in the industry started building competitive models, and a virtual wide-body price war quickly developed.

Another successful innovation first made its appearance during the mid-1990s but was slow to catch on, both in the industry and among RV consumers. That innovation was actually a sort of re-introduction of the ultra-lightweight travel trailers that were originally built to cope with the gasoline shortages and downsized automobiles of the early 1980s. The timing of the new lightweights was ideal because by the year 2000, the automobile market was being dominated by minivans and expanded lines of sports-utility vehicles, and mot of those vehicles were able to tow the lightweights.

By 2000, virtually every major RV company was producing some version of lightweight trailer, both with and without folding trailer-style end bunks and with lengths ranging from 14 to 27 feet. Although the dealers stocked those units carefully at first, by 2000 it appeared clear that there was excellent profits in retailing large numbers of the lightweights, so dealers inventoried them heavily.

The escalating gasoline prices which hit motorhome sales hard also had a significant impact on the lightweight market because, as sales declined, lot inventories remained too high. The result was widespread discounting of lightweight towables in the spring of 2001, making a whole new type of bargain available to retail customers from coast to coast! As this was written, inventories of the lightweights were still high in most parts of the country, and it appeared bargains in those units would be available through at least part of the 2002 model year.

When RV companies set out to recoup their sales following a slow economic period, or when they set their sights on increasing their market shares by out-pricing their competitors, a wide range of bargain programs are made available to dealers and consumers. Programs may take the form of manufacturer rebates, low-interest loans, free extended warranties and any number of other sales-generating offers.

I was employed at Holiday Rambler in 1988, for example, when we created a retail rebate program designed to generate sales of our most expensive models. Promoted as part of the company's 35th anniversary observance, the program pledged a $1,953 cash rebate in honor of Holiday Rambler's founding in 1953. During the rebate period, anyone who purchased one of our high-end RVs from a dealer's existing inventory was entitled to $1,953 if the dealer, in turn, replaced that unit with a new one. The program was quite successful for dealers and generated definite bargains for buyers that year, but I really have my doubts that it produced enough incremental sales to compensate the company for its phenomenal cost.

A few years later, when I headed marketing at Newmar Corporation, we used a similar program to convince current owners of Holiday Rambler products to switch to Newmar's Kountry Aire and London Aire models. We mailed a $2,000 rebate offer directly to several thousand Holiday Rambler customers, telling them we'd pay them the special rebate if they switched brands. Some two dozen families switched, generating more than $1 million in income for Newmar but giving our easy-going president worrisome second thoughts every time he had to sign a $2,000 check!

Rebates of that magnitude are rare, but they are offered from time to time, and shoppers who take advantage of them receive financial benefits that are not otherwise available.

From time to time, producers of low-cost RVs develop major price-reduction programs designed to convince shoppers to buy new, basically equipped motorhomes or trailers instead of used units. Those programs often seem to breed competition, and it is not unusual for three or four competing manufacturers to advertise similar programs at the same time. Obviously, families in the market for bargain-priced RVs are the direct beneficiaries when these programs hit the marketplace.

MARKETPLACE TRENDS

Similarly, brief marketplace trends periodically prompt RV companies to become more aggressive about promoting and selling their mid-priced or high-end brands, and during such periods, plenty of bargains can be found. It seems to me at times that every three or four years, the folding trailer manufacturers rediscover their own high-end models and decide they can make a major impact on the market by lowering their prices. Not coincidentally, that's just about the time we in the media are being told that the current crop of folding trailer customers are not first-time owners but, instead, veteran RVers who are either multiple owners of fold-outs or older couples who have switched from motorhomes and travel trailers to a simpler form of camping vehicle!

An industry-wide movement in 1994 toward upscale aluminum-frame travel trailers and fifth-wheels (see Chapter 7) resulted in a highly competitive atmosphere that forced manufacturers and their dealers to offer those coaches to consumers for excellent bargain prices. Similar competition among producers of luxury-class motorhomes (in the $250,000 range) and among builders of mid-priced diesel pusher motorhomes (costing about $150,000) has trimmed per-unit profits by at least half since 1990 and created opportunities for families to own expensive RVs that otherwise they would not be able to afford.

Shoppers should be sure to watch development of the latest RV industry trends because frequently they signal a new

round of price-cutting and marketing aggressiveness.
Manufacturers operate with a jump-on-the-bandwagon mental-
ity and consistently try to increase their market shares by riding along with the most successful new trends, offering dealers
special prices for stocking those new units. Three cases in
point: the proliferation of mid-priced wide-body (100-inch-
wide) RVs of all types; low-priced bus-style Class A
motorhomes aimed at first-time buyers, and the new ultra-light
towables aimed at SUV and mini-van owners.

Periodically the industry becomes so caught up in a marketplace trend that it over-produces and under-sells a specific
type of product, and as demand for those units declines, dealers are forced to discount them in order to meet cash-flow
needs. That's what has happened with the new crop of lightweight trailers -- manufacturers over-produced and dealers
over-stocked, resulting in an unexpected round of price-cutting
nation-wide. Obviously, by simply waiting until a trend runs its
course, shoppers can sometimes take advantage of once-in-a-
lifetime bargains. Another example was the nation-wide boom
in pickup truck camper sales during the early 1990s. Stories
about dealers' successes with pickup campers ran rampant
through the industry, encouraging others to stock their lots
with several models, only to discover they could not sell them
as quickly as they thought because their markets were already
glutted with units.

An irony of these marketplace trends is that often, a particular type of unit that retails well nation-wide will not sell at all
well in one part of the country or the other. Pickup campers, for
example, are quite popular in Colorado but sell very poorly in
New York. Thus, an astute buyer living in the Northeast might

be able to find a good bargain on a truck camper by shopping New York dealerships and looking for units that dealers want to dump. At the same time, residents of Colorado might be able to find truck camper bargains for exactly the opposite reason-- intense competition that results in lower prices!

5

GETTING THE BEST DEAL

Negotiating the best deal possible for a new or used recreational vehicle often depends upon being ready to buy at exactly the time and place that bargains are available. As we saw in Chapter 4, even an astute shopper needs to be armed with timely information about current prices. Sometimes, finding potential bargains is easier than negotiating good deals for them. In this chapter, we'll offer numerous tips on how to get the best deal on your RV purchase, but first, let's review a few key points to finding bargains:

•Try to buy your RV during the off-season, when the prices are generally lower.

•Other good times to find bargains are just prior to a model changeover and during RV shows.

•Try to learn as much as you can about the discounts, rebates, low-interest loans, free extended warranties and other price-related programs that have short-term impacts on RV prices in your locale.

•Watch for advertised special offers on RVs equipped with optional packages such as awnings, air conditioners, microwave ovens, TV antennas, etc.

•Remember that prices on specific models depend largely upon their current popularity within your local marketplace as well as how they fit into prevailing local or national trends.

Most often, you'll find the best deal for nearly any RV model that fits your family's needs by shopping in a highly competitive environment. Model selection is nearly always better in areas where dealerships are aggressively competitive with each other and where they are heavily stocked with product. At the same time, keep in mind that an outlying dealership might be willing to provide you with the best price because of its low overhead; model selection probably will not be as good, however.

Be aware that advertised RV sales prices nearly always reflect the dealer's calculation that a trade-in may be involved. The price you pay for an RV if you don't have a trade-in will usually be less than the price if you *have* a trade-in.

Don't be overly concerned about negotiating the highest possible trade-in allowance; be more concerned with the difference you will pay. If you are not satisfied with the difference offered by the dealer, the dealer can find ways to lower it -- by reducing the price of the unit you're buying or by increasing your trade-in allowance.

Before you begin to negotiate, prepare yourself mentally to walk away. Even when you find an RV that seems to fit all your needs, if you believe the price is too high or you are uncomfortable about any aspect of the sale, resolve to halt discussions and go home. Chances are, you'll find as good a unit -- and maybe even a better one -- later, and your determination to walk away could even result in important concessions being offered by the seller.

When you look at a new or used RV for the first time, do not take a checkbook or cash with you -- not even $10! That way, you cannot be pushed into making a deposit based on impulse. Don't ever give in to warnings that another prospect is quite interested in the RV but a deposit will hold it until you make up your mind.

Be wary of a sales person who refuses to talk price with you but instead, focuses on monthly payments. Negotiating on the basis of payments can obscure the true cost of the RV, allowing the salesman to talk in terms of $300 per month instead of the $15,000 price of the RV. If the salesman continues to emphasize $300 per month, pull a hand calculator out of your pocket and multiply $300 by 60 months and then emphasize that he's asking you to pay $18,000 for an RV that should cost $15,000. That's when the real price negotiations can begin. Monthly payments also can be used by a salesman to obscure the fact that the optional air conditioner he wants to sell you for $16.67 per month will cost you an extra $1,000 over the 60-month RV financing period.

The salesman who also insists that you "Make me an offer" or tell him exactly how much you are willing to spend will, I promise, find an RV for exactly that price, even if it is not what you want. Make the salesman come up with a starting figure; if he won't quote one for you, ask to speak with the manager or owner. If you aren't told a price then, leave.

On the other hand, once you are given a price, either by a dealer or a private individual, don't feel you have to accept it as a final, non-negotiable figure. When you're ready, make an offer for a price that you think is reasonable. While I usually recommend that a shopper base his offer to a dealer at a level that allows the dealership a fair profit, the fact is, during slow sales periods, a dealer might be willing to accept a break-even price merely in order to help his cash flow or open inventory space on a crowded sales lot. *So don't be embarrassed about suggesting a price that even you believe is probably too low.* For reasons you cannot know, the dealer might find that dirt-cheap price acceptable! Again, if you offer a low-profit figure and the dealer accepts it, be ready to make the purchase; don't go shopping elsewhere for an even better deal.

Used RVs sold from an individual's front yard are almost always priced on the basis of two factors: One, what the seller thinks RV dealers are asking for similar units, and two, what he paid for the unit. Individuals don't often hope to profit by selling their RVs, but they usually want to come as close as possible to breaking even. That means their asking price is somewhat arbitrary and, in my view, always open to negotiation.

NEGOTIATING PRICE

Therefore, when buying a used RV from an individual, don't feel you have to accept the person's "firm" asking price. Consider making an offer that is about 20 per cent lower than the asking price. If that offer is refused, ask the seller to make a counter offer. If he declines to do that and insists that his asking price is firm, give him your telephone number and be prepared to look elsewhere unless you find the asking price acceptable. You'll be surprised how often you'll get a follow-up telephone call from a seller after he has had a little more time to think about your offer.

When considering either a new or a used RV being sold by a dealership, ask if there is a service warranty on the unit, and if you are told there is not, ask if the dealership will guarantee the unit and its appliances for a period of time.

If you make an offer for an RV, make it in writing just as you would submit an offer when you buy a house. Include conditions of the sale and specify that the seller must check you out on the unit to your satisfaction before final payment is made.

Do not give the seller a deposit until you are absolutely certain you want to buy the unit. And that decision should be made only after you are satisfied about every aspect of the deal.

Remember our discussions about price in Chapter 2 and, when negotiating with an RV dealer, ask him to show you either the *Kelley Blue Book* or *NADA Appraisal Guide* wholesale price of the model that interests you. Every reputable dealership will have a current copy of one of those books, listing wholesale prices for RVs in rough, average or excellent condition. They also list the bank loan values and what the RV sold for when new. If you want to check *Blue Book* prices privately, most large libraries have fairly up to date copies available in their research sections, and they also are available on the Internet. Keep in mind that the condition of the RV is open to interpretation. A unit the dealer claims is in excellent condition might impress you as being in rough or average shape. Base your price negotiations upon *your* evaluation of condition, not the dealer's.

WHAT'S WRONG WITH IT?

After you've inspected the RV that interests you most (see Chapter 6), you should have a list of its shortcomings. Use that list to begin bargaining. If you feel the price quoted to you is unacceptable, you should ask that all the problem areas be corrected at no cost. Typically, the dealer will be willing to correct some problems but not others. He is unlikely to hesitate replacing burned out taillights, for example, and he'll probably touch up a paint scratch, but he might not be willing to repair a dented body or replace a damaged screendoor. I believe it is perfectly acceptable for your offer to be conditional upon replacement of damaged lightbulbs or cracked windows and repair of items such as electrical switches, ceiling vents, cabinet latches and locks. When negotiating with a private individual, it also is reasonable if you ask that the sale include items already in the unit such as a paper towel holder, mounted radio, clock and electrical hookup adapter plug.

Consider informing a dealer that if you buy his RV, you will need to add accessories to it. Give him a list of those and ask him to provide you with a package price for the items, perhaps including a new refrigerator, an awning or an air conditioner. Then negotiate a service contract; ask for a dealership warranty covering a 90-day period after the sale, but be aware that the best terms you'll probably get is for 30 days.

Tell the dealer that if you buy the unit, you expect it to be cleaned inside and outside, with LP tanks and gasoline tank (if it's a motorhome) filled with fuel. Also insist that appliances be operated in your presence so that you can make certain they work properly. Then ask the dealer to pay the state sales tax and maybe even replace the RV's battery and tires.

Finally, point out to the dealer that if you buy his RV, you will need camping gear in order to use it; ask him to provide you with a parts store package that includes a sewer hose, water hose, campground directory, electrical cord adapter plug, water pressure regulator and extension cord. You might not convince him to give you everything you've requested. But on the other hand, he might just do it! And you certainly won't get it if you don't ask for it.

A final condition to the sale should be an orientation period in which the seller explains the RV's entire operation to you: how to light the water heater; how to empty the holding tanks; how to fill the water tank; how to replace fuses and find the circuit breakers; how the exterior step operates; how and where to turn on the water pump; how the monitor panel operates; how to turn on the air conditioner, refrigerator, furnace and generator, and how to extend and retract the awning.

If, after all this, you agree to buy the RV and the seller accepts your check, you can expect to hear a loud sigh of relief from him as you drive away because you've proven to be one *tough* customer!

6
LET'S GO RV SHOPPING

Going shopping for an RV should not mean leaving your house with a checkbook, ready to buy the first coach that seems to meet your needs. First, you should prepare for your actual day of purchase by educating yourself on what's available in the marketplace. I recommend the following steps:

ONE -- Check the ads in your local newspapers and in national and regional RV magazines to get a good picture of the products that are currently being offered for sale and the prices that are being asked for those products. Consider investing in a copy of *Trailer Life* magazine's annual RV buyer's guide (available at most large magazine stores).

TWO -- Determine which types and brands of RVs interest you most and write to manufacturers of those units for literature.

THREE -- Visit local RV dealerships, preferably when they are closed, to determine the types, brands and prices of RVs being stocked locally.

FOUR -- If a local RV show or travel/vacation show where RVs are displayed is being held locally, attend it so that you can examine a broad range of the units that interest you most.

FIVE -- If an RV factory is near your home, or if you intend to travel to an area where an RV factory is located, try schedule a plant tour so that you can get a first-hand look at how RVs are built.

SIX -- Meanwhile, either begin making a checklist of the features, accessories and options that are most important to your family or use the one we've provided for you (Appendix I, Features Checklist) in the back of this book. We recommend that you make copies of the checklist and use a different sheet each time you examine an RV that interests you. Compare the items on it with the amenities offered on the various RVs you find appealing. A second list is a good idea, too; it can be limited to *unusual* features available in various models -- spice rack, trash storage bin, room divider, icemaker, shoe storage rack, entertainment center, stereo sound system, self-storing tables, lift-up beds, central air conditioning, roof storage pod, insulated water and holding tanks, heated basement storage space, combination gas/electric water heater.

SEVEN -- Finally, develop a rating system --perhaps a numbered 5-scale or 10-scale -- that can be used between now and the time you make your final choice to assign ratings to each of the models you are considering. (We've provided an Impressions Checklist, Appendix III in the back of this book, to help you do this.) Rate each RV unit on your shopping list according to your impressions and the following criteria:

- Price
- Quality
- Serviceability
- Resale value
- Performance (towability or handling)
- Construction
- Equipment and features

- •Floorplan
- •Storage space
- •Reputation and reliability of the dealership
- •Reputation of the manufacturer
- •How the RV seems to fit your needs (for weekends, vacations, long trips, short trips, seasonally, off-road boondocking, long-term or full-time living).

By this point, you should be able to begin paring down your alternative RV types, brands and models and start zeroing in on units that will fit your needs. Now you're almost ready to go RV shopping. First, let's review some basics about sleeping space and storage space.

SLEEPING SPACE

This is a basic requirement that, on the surface, does not seem to deserve much discussion because everyone knows an RV should have enough bunk space for everyone in the family. In actual fact, however, ***bed sizes, types and arrangements present RV buyers with difficult choices***. Except for folding camping trailers and pickup campers, most RVs can be equipped with twin beds, double beds, queen-size beds and sometimes, even king-size beds. There are bunk beds, stacked bunks and walk-around island beds. There are convertible dinettes, sofa/beds, cabinet bunks, swing-down bunks and gaucho/bunks. The most popular RV floorplans contain at least one permanent bed (usually in a rear bedroom) and convertible dinettes and sofas that serve double duty for sitting and sleeping. Walk-around island beds are more popular than beds that are placed flush against walls, and they add to an RV's resale value. Queen-size beds have better resale appeal than double beds. Gauchos, swing-down bunks (primarily in Class A motorhomes) and cabinet bunks are a few years out of fashion due to comfort shortcomings. Stacked (or criss-crossed) bunks are popular for families with three or more children.

STORAGE SPACE

An unfortunate current trend in RV construction is to reduce costs by eliminating desirable cabinet space. Reducing the number of overhead cabinets, particularly in a travel trailer's front living room and rear bedroom areas, has the added effect of making the coach appear to be more spacious. But loss of that storage space can prove to be a serious handicap on camping trips and vacations. RV buyers also should be wary of overhead cabinets in kitchens that are narrower than usual; cabinets there that are too narrow for standard 10-inch dinner plates can prove to be quite troublesome. When shopping for an RV, take the time to note whether overheads are available everywhere they ought to be and whether the cabinets are wide enough for your needs, whether they are equipped with shelves and dividers and whether the doors close tightly enough to prevent stored items from falling out during travel.

A kitchen's undersink area should provide good, usable space and not just be a dark, open hole containing a bird's nest of wiring and plumbing lines. The compartment should be equipped with at least one shelf to hold pots and pans, and ideally, it should be lighted -- although few RV manufacturers go to the trouble or expense to provide that feature. Two or more drawers for eating utensils and small kitchen items should be provided. The RV should also have either a pantry or a cabinet area for storing food, particularly canned goods.

Somewhere in the RV, preferably in the undersink area, should be a place for keeping trash. And another storage space (most likely in the bathroom) is needed for laundry. The bathroom also should be equipped with a mirrored-door medicine cabinet large enough to contain all the usual bathroom items, and the bathroom undersink area ought to be spacious enough for at least a few rolls of tissue and bottles of holding tank deodorant.

It is not usually necessary for an RV to feature a full-length closet because most RVers do not take floor-length coats or long dresses camping with them. Women who are active square-dancers and wear full skirts might need that type of space, however. Be sure there is a closet storage section, preferably near floor level, for shoes, slippers and shower thongs, though. The closet should have an eye-level shelf for storing hats, sweaters and other clothing.

In the bedroom, overhead shelves are needed for clothing, and half-length shirt closets (usually placed either at the foot of a bed or above one or more nightstands) are quite useful, although not always provided. The bed or beds should be hinged so they lift with the help of gas struts for access to underbed storage spaces; those areas are excellent places for keeping extra blankets, sheets, pillows or items such as heavy coats which might not be used often. The most useful nightstands are those with multiple drawers, although most feature only one drawer above an open storage space.

Outside, the ideal RV should have storage compartments for odd-shaped items such as the sewer hose, lawn chairs, fishing rods, water hose, electric extension cords, a toolbox and a barbecue grill. RVs with basements provide excellent storage spaces but are quite easy to overload. Some basement areas are equipped with pull-out storage drawers and special features such as a slide-out barbecue grill or picnic table.

Most new RVs are not equipped with roof storage pods, but many used units have them. Pods are especially good for storing off-season or seldom used items. Authors Ron and Barb Hofmeister regarded an *"attic"* pod as indispensable when they started full-time RVing in a small motorhome. In their book, *Movin' On*, they wrote, "Items stored in our attic were winter clothes, lantern, tennis rackets, rain gear, decorative lights, a one-foot-tall decorated Christmas tree and plastic air mattresses for lounging in pools. We also stored flat, soft-type luggage, fishing gear, a smaller cooler and golf clubs."

REMEMBER THE BATHROOM

When shopping for an RV, it's easy to be influenced by advice that you should concentrate on models that provide the appropriate amount of sleeping, dining, meal preparation, storage and closet space for your family. Those aspects are, indeed, important. But while you're focusing your attention on those areas, don't allow yourself to neglect features and equipment that could make the difference between being comfortable or miserable on a camping trip.

For example, *the most under-rated area in an RV is its bathroom.* First-time buyers tend to ignore the size and features of RV bathrooms, only to learn later that they spend more time in those tiny spaces than they thought they would. Veteran RVers consistently rank bathroom size, location, layout and features as among the most important considerations in their purchase of a new unit.

In fact, I would be willing to bet that a significant proportion of the late-model used RVs for sale on dealers' lots were traded in on new ones because their owners judged the bathrooms to be inadequate.

The most criticized features of RV bathrooms, besides size, are the inconvenient location of a toilet, the lack of storage space for toiletries and the poor design of shower stalls. I'll never forget the anger expressed by a friend who examined a motorhome's toilet compartment and complained, "I could do my business in there okay, but I'd have to go out into the hall for the paperwork."

Bathtubs and shower areas are notoriously poorly designed and constructed. Many of the most widely used models of combination tub/showers require the camper to balance on one foot and climb into them through a child-size opening. Frequently, the showers are made of thin ABS plastic with inadequately reinforced walls and floors; cracks in the plastic are common.

A few manufacturers, recognizing an easy way to cut corners and build bottom-line profits, have all but eliminated bathroom storage space except for a shelved hole under the sink and a tiny, cheap mirrored-door medicine cabinet on one wall. I suspect the reason there are so many used RVs with those features on dealers' lots is that they have been dumped by camping families who realize they need better bathrooms.

While walking through a new or used RV that interests you, consider whether the bathroom has adequate storage space for your family's toiletries and whether it has towel racks, a large enough mirror and heating ducts. Either the bathroom should have space for keeping towels and linens or there ought to be a linen closet conveniently located nearby. Is the tub/shower large enough, and is its closure feature (curtain or sliding door) adequate? In order to step into the tub, do you have to climb over the toilet or stand on a heating register? Is the shower enclosure well built or does it look as if it leaks? Stand in the shower to determine if the space there is adequate. Does the bathroom have a built-in hamper for dirty clothes? Is there enough knee and elbow room when seated on the toilet? Does the bathroom have -- and do you need -- a power roof vent?

ITEM-BY-ITEM INSPECTION

Now, as you walk through the rest of the RV, use your checklist to indicate whether the unit meets your item-by-item needs. If it lacks a feature, make note of that; as the number of shortcomings increases, it should become clear to you that a particular model is not the RV for you and your family.

•**Do cabinet doors latch** to your satisfaction? Do drawers open and close smoothly? Is there enough storage space for food, cookware, eating utensils, clothing, coats, linens and bedding? Is closet or drawer space sufficient for storing shoes, underwear, socks and hanging clothes?

•**Rate the cross-ventilation** and the amount of lighting. Are there enough reading lights, and are they conveniently placed? Is the galley area well illuminated? Is the light in the bathroom satisfactory? Check the number and locations of electrical outlets.

•**Evaluate the unit's decor** -- its color scheme, the design of patterns on the upholstery, the type of window treatment provided, the quality of fabrics, the type of floor covering. If you are shopping for a new RV, remember that you can usually order a unit built with decor features and colors you like. If you are shopping for a used unit, keep in mind the replacement costs of features you don't like as well as whether those features will help or hinder you when you're ready to resell the unit.

•**No matter what type** or size RV you buy, it ought to be equipped with a deadbolt lock. All towable RVs should have safety chains. Every unit (except a truck camper, of course) should have a spare tire and jack. Is there space in the RV for a TV set? Or a radio? Or a portable microwave oven? If those accessories are important to you, make sure your RV has convenient places to put them.

•**Check the condition** of the galley sink. Is it stainless steel or porcelain? Stainless steel is more expensive but tends to discolor easily; porcelain will chip easier. Also, inspect the fit of the sink into the countertop. Many models of inexpensive porcelain sinks have natural warps and are difficult to install, even by factory experts. Is there enough kitchen countertop space for family meal preparation? Where will you put your trash? Can the kitchen floor be kept clean easily?

•**Check the windows.** Are they sliders or awning-type? Awning or jalousie windows provide better ventilation, especially during rains, but the awning mechanisms sometimes do not operate properly. Veteran RVers prefer awning windows in bedrooms, but not necessarily in living areas. Awning windows provide better security than sliders. If you're examining a used RV, make certain the window frames are well sealed, and check for evidence of leaks around the windows. Do the windows latch securely?

•**Examine the RV's heating ducts.** Ductwork routed through the floor is more expensive than ducting through cabinetry, and it usually -- but not always -- provides better temperature control. Cabinet ductwork nearly always takes up valuable storage space.

•**Are the furnace and water heater** equipped with electronic ignitions or must they be lighted with matches? If you plan to do any winter or cold-weather camping, determine how well the RV water lines are protected from outside temperatures. Are water line cutoff valves conveniently located? In used RVs, look for evidence of plumbing leaks under sinks, in the tub and in base-level storage compartments where water lines are routed. Check the sizes of waste tanks, water tanks, propane and gasoline tanks. In used units, look inside cabinets and under bunks for evidence of dust leaks.

•**Check the seating** -- the sofa, chairs, dinette -- for comfort. Lie down on the bed. If the RV has a convertible sofa/bed or gaucho, test its comfort in its multiple configurations. Is there storage space under the dinette, and is there access to it without removing the dinette cushions? Is the dinette roomy enough or was it designed for children and not full-figured adults?

•**Examine the appliances** and determine whether they are large enough for your family. For example, do you need a large refrigerator with a separate freezer compartment? Do you need a cooking range with combination oven or would you prefer a rangetop and a separate microwave oven?

Most importantly with a used RV, examine it closely throughout for water leaks. Look at the walls, the ceilings, the baseboards and even inside the cabinets. Stains, freshly painted surfaces and replaced sections of wall or ceilings often indicate presence -- either past or current -- of water damage, due most often to roof leaks.

Climb up on the roof and look for damage there as well as for low spots, loose seams and potential problem areas around vents and the air conditioner. Then check underneath the rig, looking for welds or other repairs that might indicate structural damage.

APPLIANCE REPAIR/REPLACEMENT

Unless you are able to buy your new or used RV at a truly bargain price, I strongly recommend that you avoid purchasing a unit with appliances that you plan to replace or repair. Consider this:

•Repairing an RV refrigerator probably will cost you between $200 and $700, and replacing it could mean shelling out up to $2,000.

•Repairing a water heater could cost you $150, and a replacement model runs between $350 and $700.

•Repairing an RV's furnace might mean spending only $50-$100, but a replacement is likely to cost between $450 and $800.

•Repairing an RV range probably will cost up to $100 even though an entirely new model may be priced at only $200-250.

•Repairing an RV's toilet could cost nearly as much as an entirely new replacement model.

Also keep in mind that appliance repairs might be little more than short-term fixes and that even more -- and perhaps more expensive -- repairs could very well be required in the future. Repairing a refrigerator by replacing its compressor, for example, is no guarantee that the appliance's cooling unit won't need to be replaced too, so an initial repair job that costs only $200 might be nothing more than the first of $1,000 worth of service work.

Obviously, the family buying a used travel trailer for $4,000 does not want to be hit immediately with another $1,000-3,000 outlay in order to make that RV's appliances operable. On the other hand, a family that already owns an RV should consider whether they are better off buying a new coach, with its all-new appliances, rather than risking potentially major appliance repair expenses if they keep their current unit.

One often-ignored reality of RV ownership is that even-
tually, most appliances will need to be replaced.

Veteran RV service companies calculate the life-expectancy of an appliance at 10 years. If that seems to be a very short operable period, consider not only that most home appliances have life-expectancies of only seven years, but also that RV appliances are subjected to unusual vibrations, bumps and environmental conditions that do not face home-type products.

The meaning is clear: Every RV owner should make plans either to spend money for replacing his appliances eventually or he should count on trading RVs before appliance replacements become necessary.

Most of our friends who are full-time RVers or snowbirds tend to plan for the eventuality of replacing their appliances. They include the cost of those replacements in their budgets and set aside small amounts of cash each month for repairs and replacements. Then, when an appliance stops operating satisfactorily, they consider whether to have it repaired or invest in an entirely new model.

Tom Griffin, a widely recognized RV service expert who is an RVer himself, insists that as an appliance approaches its 10-year life-expectancy, replacement should be more of a consideration than repairs. For many years, Griffin was a factory service representative at the Holiday Rambler Corporation, and during that time, he saw numerous examples of families that decided to spend hundreds of dollars for repairs, only to be faced with even more expensive service work a few months later. He is convinced replacing appliances rather than repairing them often is the better choice.

Griffin also points out that today's electronic appliances are so technologically complicated that most do-it-yourself mechanics are not able to make the repairs themselves, and even highly skilled RV service center technicians frequently have difficulty determining exactly why an appliance is not operating properly.

If an RV furnace is not lighting, for example, the first thought of most technicians is that its electronic circuit board probably needs to be replaced. But the furnace could also have other problems, so simply replacing the board might not be the solution. In that case, several hours could be spent -- at the rate of $30-100 per hour -- tracking down what's really wrong. In the end, a more economical solution might have been to replace the entire furnace.

DO-IT-YOURSELF REPAIR?

In theory, there are some appliance repairs that can be made easily by do-it-yourselfers. If an appliance's LP-gas burner is not operating properly, for example, a skilled amateur mechanic might be able to take apart the burner and clean it,

saving himself a substantial amount of money. But unfortunately, most RV owner's manuals do not include instructions
on how to do that simple work because, for legal reasons, manufacturers do not want to encourage do-it-yourself repairs on
sensitive LP-gas components.

Partly as a consequence of these handicaps, today's RV
appliances have become throw-away products rather than re-
pairable ones. It is easier -- and in many cases less time consuming and expensive -- to replace an entire appliance instead
of repairing it.

But even the process of appliance replacement has its difficulties.

Replacement models are readily available for all major-
brand appliances. Some appliance manufacturers, in fact, earn
more money building replacements than they do in producing
factory-installed models. Sizes, features and even connections
are relatively standard today, so that a factory-installed Magic
Chef range can be replaced quite easily with a Wedgewood; a
SeaLand toilet will fit the same space as a Thetford unit; a
Norcold refrigerator can be installed in place of a Dometic
model.

However, replacement is often not simply a matter of
removing the old appliance and dropping in a new one. Because most of today's RVs are built *around* the appliances,
removing a furnace or refrigerator can be quite difficult and
time consuming. And when an RV owner is faced with paying
$50 an hour or more in labor costs, that time can quickly
become very expensive.

I know of mechanically inclined RV owners who have tried
to save money by removing their old appliances themselves,

but in most cases, they've admitted later they wished they had not done it.

Before a refrigerator can be removed, for example, it should be drained of freon. That process alone is somewhat complicated, but then after the freon is drained, the RV owner must find some way to dispose of it. Once the LP-gas and electric lines are disconnected -- a difficult job in itself -- some way must be found to remove the refrigerator from inside the RV.

Typically, most RV refrigerators weigh about 150 pounds and are very tough appliances to lift and carry. And, they are too tall, wide and deep to fit through an RV's entry door. In most cases, large windows must be removed in order to lift them out of the RV.

Furnaces that have been installed under the bench seats of dinette/bunks offer are especially challenging to replace. Often, the dinette itself has to be either dismantled or destroyed in order to remove the furnace.

Disconnecting LP-gas and electric lines from appliances such as refrigerators can also present difficulties to the do-it-yourselfer, according to the owner of Tech Works RV Service Specialists in Elkhart, Indiana. He said he often has to complete disconnection work started and "screwed up" by RV owners who try to save themselves money.

SHORTAGE OF TECHNICIANS

On the other hand, a nation-wide shortage of skilled RV technicians currently presents RV owners with a series of unique problems: Shops which employ good appliance service personnel are difficult to find in some sections of the country, and even when they can be found, they frequently are quite specialized in the types of work they are willing to do. A developing trend, for example, is that many RV appliance centers refuse to perform repairs of any kind except for replacing circuit boards, igniters and refrigerator compressors or cooling units. Typically, they refer all appliance repair work to another company -- for a fee that the customer ends up paying.

And, while RV travelers have traditionally relied on RV retail dealerships for their service work, the shortage of technicians has prevented many dealers from recruiting the talent they need, so appliance repair/replacement work sometimes is performed by untrained service personnel who literally must learn everything while they are working.

In searching for a service center to handle his appliance repair or replacement work, the RV traveler quickly learns he is unable to shop around for the best prices; often, he can regard himself as fortunate if he can find a service center that is able and willing to do the work at any price. More and more service centers are announcing they are not interested in doing upgrade repair or replacement work simply because they are focusing all their efforts on highly lucrative factory warranty service.

Another potentially important aspect of the repair-replacement process is the availability of replacement RVs with features that were not offered on older models. For example, it might make sense for you to replace an old piezo-ignition refrigerator or a match-lighted furnace with direct-spark, electronic-ignition models. Also, a new refrigerator probably will be more spacious inside than an older model of the same size. Most of today's furnaces have higher btu-output than similar models built ten years ago. Or perhaps it's time to replace an old LP-fueled water heater with a gas/electric model that fits into the same size space.

OTHER APPLIANCE REPLACEMENTS

Along with refrigerators, air conditioners are among the most expensive RV appliances to replace, but repairs to them can quite often be made without a substantial investment. A typical low-profile 13,500-btu replacement air conditioner with manual controls, a three-speed blower and an optional 5,600-btu heat strip will cost approximately $700 plus installation fees. But that type unit can be installed rather easily and quickly; costs escalate when ACs with automatic features and wall-mounted thermostats are purchased. Those cost $800-$1,000. On the other hand, most AC manufacturers offer basic, no-frills models rated for 7,500 btu that cost just over $500.

Replacing a toilet is relatively inexpensive, although finding a technician to do the work sometimes can be difficult. The most common replacement toilet is Thetford's Aqua-Magic IV, available in either foot-pedal flush or hand flush; cost, about $120. Thetford's Starlite model, with *"homelike"* features such as an elongated and contoured seat and enlarged bowl, are about $170 but can be found for around $130. The homelike Galaxie, an upgrade model with a padded lid, generally cost about $190 but are available for $40 less.

The SeaLand Traveler 510 china toilet has a residential size bowl that accepts regular home-size replacement seats. Primarily a replacement unit, it retails for about $200. The Traveler 910, featuring a self-cleaning flush ball with Teflon seal that the manufacturer claims locks out odors, is about $170.

When replacing a kitchen sink, figure on spending about $60-80 for a self-rimmed, stainless steel single-bowl model and $90-140 for a double stainless steel type. Keep in mind that porcelain sinks usually cost less, but they warp easily and are often quite difficult to install. Kitchen faucets range from $25 for a four-inch center ledge model to $50 for an eight-inch single-lever type; bathroom faucets are $16-35.

SHURflo replacement water pumps cost $90-155 for multi-fixture demand models; PAR-Mate automatic 12-volt pumps for small RVs are $100; for larger coaches, $140; Jabsco demand pumps cost $160-210.

When buying replacement appliances from RV dealers, expect to spend up to $600 for a U-Line icemaker; $450 for a built-in 1.2-cubic-foot Magic Chef microwave oven ($360 for a .8-cubic-foot model); $85 for a Ventline power range hood; $375 for an AC/DC 10-inch color TV set; $400 for an AC/DC video cassette player; $120-220 for a power converter, and $100-$210 for a roof-mounted TV antenna.

MAKING THE DECISION

Here is the methodology I recommend to someone considering whether to repair or replace an appliance:

ONE -- Find a nearby service center that has a good reputation for performing quality repair or installation work.

TWO -- Determine how much the replacement appliance costs.

THREE -- Ask the service center how much it typically charges to replace the type of appliance you need.

FOUR -- Ask the service center to examine your RV's appliance and give you a repair-cost estimate.

FIVE -- Compare the appliance cost and replacement cost against the estimated cost of repairing the appliance and determine which option is better for your situation. Consider the age of the appliance in terms of how close it is to its expected life-span of 10 years.

AWNINGS AND SCREEN ROOMS

Make no mistake: A new or used RV equipped with an awning is a better buy than one without it. Adding an awning is not only expensive, both in terms of its price and its installation cost, but finding a service center to install one inexpensively and competently can be quite difficult.

Once considered luxury accessories that were nice to have but unnecessary and expensive, today's RV awnings are rapidly becoming regarded as critical to many families' RVing lifestyles. Awnings, in fact, have already evolved into standard accessories on a wide range of RV brands; not only are they now routinely factory-installed, but they also are commonly *"packaged"* along with other popular accessories and then sold by dealerships for considerably less than they would otherwise cost if they were bought separately from the RV and then installed on it.

Screen rooms -- once little more than flimsy structures meant to protect families from flying insects at mealtime -- are rapidly moving into the realm of being extensions of an RV's living areas. Better built than ever before, yet also easier to erect and take down, they are now designed either to stand alone or to connect directly to an RV's awning roll bar. They are being used as outdoor living rooms, nurseries, kitchens, lounges, party rooms and even bedrooms!

Here is another good reason for buying an RV with an awning already installed: Because of elevating aluminum costs and higher demand for awnings during the last few years, prices are gradually increasing, and adding an awning to a new or used RV that does not have one is a major expense for most families.

Conversely, the same kinds of price pressures are not being felt by manufacturers of screen rooms. Instead, while demand is improving, competition for the larger number of buyers is increasing too, and that very competition should result in level, and in some case lower, prices over the next couple of years. Ironically, the bottom-line prices paid by consumers for screen rooms could, in the final analysis, be higher than ever simply because families are ordering larger, better built screen rooms with more features. And, in many cases, the screen rooms purchased are ordered custom-built to fit specific families' RVs.

BETTER RESALE VALUE?

Increased popularity of awnings and screen rooms is definitely having its affect on the resale of used recreational vehicles. With awning demand high among RV owners from all economic levels, used travel trailers and motorhomes that are not already equipped with awnings are proving to have less resale value. On the other hand, an awning that, in itself, has only a limited amount of appeal because of its design, colors or features can actually lower the resale value of the RV on which it is installed.

Keep in mind, trends in awning colors come and go, and

you don't want the new or used RV you buy to feature a color scheme that will be badly out of style in a few years. In the 1970s, most awnings featured vertical stripes; in the 1980s, horizontal stripes were in vogue and vertical color schemes were hard to sell. For the last few years, the trend was away from solid stripes of both kinds and toward either solid colors or multi-shade gradient patterns. Now, there appears to be a developing trend toward solid earth tones with bright splashes of color similar to the graphics treatments that are increasingly popular on RV exteriors.

Colors that seem to have the strongest consumer appeal during the early 2000s are shadow-shades of teal, burgundy, blue, brown and gray rather than the distinctive stripes of the mid-1990s. Typically, the actual color ordered is chosen to match the striping or graphics of the RV on which the awning will be installed.

Woven acrylic fabric that allows bright colors to be displayed on both sides of the awning also appears to be increasing in popularity, although awnings featuring that fabric are more expensive than those with vinyl material. Most factory-installed awnings utilize vinyl.

The leading awning companies tend to focus attention one or more aspects of their business even while trying to supply product for the broadest range of uses.

CONSTRUCTION QUALITY

To give yourself a good idea about the RV's construction quality, make a quick check of the fit-and-finish in corners, at cabinet attachment points, inside cabinet doors, inside drawers, under shelves and along the inside fronts of cabinets. If the finish is rough, with finger-poking splinters, nailheads or staples, be wary; that work usually indicates a lack of quality control throughout the unit.

I'll never forget the time a friend took me on a tour of a reorganized RV manufacturing plant shortly after he became the new president. The company had, earlier, achieved a poor reputation for its fit-and-finish and quality control. As my friend proudly escorted me through some of his updated -- and admittedly beautiful -- RVs, I opened an overhead cabinet door, put my hand inside under the top shelf and was, at the same time, cut by the point of a staple and punctured under a fingernail by a large splinter. I withdrew my bleeding hand and said, "It looks to me as if your units have the same old quality that made them famous." Two days later, my friend telephoned me with information that he had just implemented a complete new quality control program.

After you've checked out a coach's interior workmanship, inspect inside the exterior storage compartments for poor quality, sloppy or inadequate weather seals and excessive use of sealant. Foam and acrylic sealer and caulking compounds are frequently used to cover poor workmanship. My oldest son once worked as an end-of-line inspector at an Indiana RV factory widely known for its high volume and poor quality. Noting that he could literally see daylight in the gap between where the ceiling and wall of a trailer were joined, he refused to allow the coach to roll off the line. The plant superintendent was called and, after examining the work, he instructed that the offending gap should be filled with foam, and then the trailer was to be sent on its way to the dealer that had ordered it. My son did as he was told but quit his job that afternoon.

Examine exterior storage compartments for their roominess. Popular exterior features include outdoor electric receptacles, cable TV or telephone jacks, roof rack and ladder, stabilizing or leveling jacks, awning, exterior lights, automatic LP-gas tank regulator (towables only). Motorhome features might also include landing lights, rearview TV monitor and towing hitch.

CHECK OUT THE WEIGHT

Learn how much the RV weighs. Its gross vehicle weight rating (GVWR) should be listed on a tag attached to the unit, but make certain the actual weight of the RV falls well below that GVWR so that you have capacity to add supplies, camping equipment and fluids. Weight is critically important in towable RVs because you do not want to invest in a trailer that is too heavy for your tow vehicle.

Most RV companies list their models' *"curb"* or *"dry"* weights in their literature. But keep in mind those weights are base figures without the addition of options such as air conditioners or generators considered. To the published weight figures, add the estimated total weight of all options, plus eight pounds per gallon for water and holding tanks in order to calculate a relatively accurate estimate of an RV's payload capacity -- its GVWR less its road weight. Any towables payload near or under 500 pounds is too slim a margin for safety. To figure a motorized RV's payload, include the weight of all passengers and eight pounds per gallon of fuel capacity.

FIRST-TIME RV BUYERS

Never before has the concept of RV ownership appealed to more people than it does today. That is because the oldest members of the so-called "Baby-Boom Generation" have reached the age at which American consumers traditionally purchase their first RVs. The vanguard of that huge 75-million population is now early middle age, and the baby-boomers who are 45 to 52 years old are making their presence felt at RV dealerships around the country.

The RV industry regards them as entry-level campers. In actual fact, a high proportion of them already are experienced campers; while in their 20s and 30s, they participated in outdoor activities such as backpacking, canoeing and tenting. They are seasoned travelers, and they are both outdoor and nature oriented.

For the most part, they are somewhat familiar with recreational vehicles. They have friends or family members who are RVers. They have slept overnight in their tents alongside RVs. They have both admired and ridiculed the comfort that an RV offers.

But now, they're ready to buy their first RVs. It's time, they say, to go camping with some of the luxuries. It's time to stop sleeping on the ground and move into a real bed. It's time to eat meals and socialize without wearing raincoats. It's time to carry food in a refrigerator, not an ice chest; to prepare meals on a countertop range, not over an open fire.

Today's new crop of entry-level RV buyers are not shopping for the same types of RVs -- or for the same reasons -- as the generation that preceded them, however. Most veteran *snowbird*-type RVers started camping several years ago because it was an economical way for their families to travel and vacation together economically; they invested in their first RVs and then moved gradually into larger, more luxurious units as their income levels increased.

Various studies of the people who represent today's new generation of entry-level RV buyers provide us with an different, and at times conflicting, general profile of them:

•They are less concerned with the cost of travel than are current RVers, but they are significantly more concerned about their own lack of travel time.

•They take shorter trips (of 3-4 days' duration) more often (4-10 times per year) than traditional RVers.

•They regard an RV not as an investment but as an expense.

•They worry that the cost of RV ownership is too high, considering the amount of use the RV would be given.

•They have less discretionary income than traditional RV purchasers, so RV affordability is of real concern to them.

•They do not understand RV financing.

Although these entry-level RV buyers currently are purchasing recreational vehicles that represent the full range of types, prices, styles and amenities, a distinct majority are choosing small, less expensive models of folding camping trailers, travel trailers, fifth-wheels, pickup campers and multi-purpose van campers.

The process of buying an entry-level camping vehicle often is more difficult than purchasing a luxury-equipped RV for full-time living, simply because most aspiring full-time RVers have accumulated several years of experience that should help them simplify their choices, whereas first-timers often make their decisions without really knowing what their cam-ping needs are.

The process is even harder for entry-level buyers who fit the typical baby-boomer profile. Because of their uncertainties about RVing and RV ownership, they tend to regard any RV purchase with caution and exhibit an unwillingness to commit substantial financial resources to a type of product that they are unconvinced they will use very often.

Although I feel those individuals will ultimately enjoy RV travel and camping much more than they believe, and that they will move quickly into larger, more expensive units, I also think a small financial commitment for an entry-level RV can provide them with an excellent taste for RV-type camping.

The average entry-level RV buyer, therefore, should focus his attention initially on a few specific types and styles of RVs:

ONE -- A small travel trailer, generally under 22 feet long, that can be towed by the family automobile, mini-van or SUV without investing in a tow truck or van.

TWO -- A small fifth-wheel trailer, up to 25 feet long, that can be towed by the family's light-duty pickup truck.

THREE -- A lightweight pickup truck camper that slides into the bed of the family's light-duty pickup truck.

FOUR -- A multiple-purpose camping van that can be utilized both for camping and around-town transportation.

FIVE -- A folding camping trailer that can be towed by the family car.

The least expensive of all these is the folding trailer, and every entry-level RV shopper should at least consider this type of unit before making his purchase. The appeal of folding camping trailers is easy to understand: They are designed and equipped to handle virtually any size family comfortably; they are easy to tow and easy to park, and they have the sort of back-to-nature image that appeals to people who aren't quite ready to go camping in vehicles equipped with icemakers and microwave ovens. They cost between $3,000 and $10,000, depending upon amenities.

Small travel trailers are more difficult to tow and store than folding trailers, but they usually feature full bathrooms, larger refrigerators, more storage space and are more ready-to-use than folding trailers. Their prices generally range from about $5,000 to $15,000.

For those who have difficulty deciding between a folding trailer and a small travel trailer, the solution might be a tele-scoping trailer such as the Hi-Lo or the TrailManor. Both offer low-profile towing, but while Hi-Lo's living area is extended by a telescoping top, the TrailManor extends outward with assistance from torsion bar lift mechanisms. Generally speaking, both trailers are more expensive than either folding trailers or standard travel trailers.

Another version of extended-top trailers has growing appeal among entry-level buyers. It is a small hard-side travel trailer, usually up to 21 feet long, with a roof that can be raised to provide stand-up interior living space. Versions are available from Sun-Lite.

Aside from those and the standard small travel trailers built by numerous RV manufacturers, a type of compact, lightweight trailer featuring a rounded fiberglass shell and aerodynamic design is produced by two companies: Evelands, Inc. (which builds Scamp) and Casita Enterprises. Both products are rather expensive for entry-level buyers, however, and so they tend to be marketed toward older couples.

Among the numerous small fifth-wheels available today, the current trend-setters are low-profile and lightweight models built by Fleetwood Enterprises (which offers Prowler, Terry and Wilderness series), Sunline Coach, Jayco, Coachmen, Starcraft, Thor, Aero Coach and R-Vision.

First-timers who do not want to tow trailers should consider either van campers or, if they already own pickup trucks, slide-in truck campers. I recommend giving first consideration to products built by Lance, Jayco, Coachmen, Starcraft and Fleetwood. Nearly a dozen companies produce camping vans that are great for shopping and touring as well as camping, and they are adequately powered for towing boats, snowmobile trailers and even small travel trailers. Among the best known of those are Roadtrek, Sportsmobile and Xplorer. Slide-in truck campers are available in either hard-wall versions or compact models with pop-top or crank-up roofs. Van campers cost from $25,000 to $60,000, while entry-level truck campers are available for $3,000 to $8,000.

FOLDING TRAILER SHOPPING

Shopping for a folding camping trailer requires a totally different mind-set than trying to buy any other kind of RV. So if a camping trailer is in your future, please heed this advice:

First, consider camper length. That's a confusing issue in itself, because manufacturers and dealers don't quite play fairly when they talk about length. At the wholesale level, they sell *"box"* length; to retail customers, they refer to *"set-up"* length. "Box" length is basically the size of the camper box in its folded-down, travel position; "set-up" length is the size of the camper in its ready-to-use campsite position. Most folding camper boxes are 8, 10, 12 and 13 or 14 feet long, with six-inch variances becoming the norm. "Set-up" lengths generally range from 17 to 24 feet, although a few shorter ones are offered too.

Next, consider weight. Like any other towable RV, your folding camping trailer should be matched to your tow vehicle, so focus only on the models that have gross vehicle weight ratings (GVWRs) comfortably below the towing rating of your tow vehicle. Keep in mind that adding optional equipment increases not only the cost of a camper, but also its weight. Adding weight also can require the addition of even more expensive options, such as brake, suspension and hitch systems.

Cost of the rig is, of course, an important consideration. Although base prices vary from a low of about $3,000 to a high of around $10,000, the most popular models are typically available for approximately $5,000.

As for models, floorplans and furnishings, my best advice continues to be this: Shop first at RV dealerships handling the three most popular brands -- Fleetwood (Coleman), Jayco and Starcraft. Those companies offer the most variety in lengths, models and equipment, and a fact of life in the RV marketplace is that every other manufacturer (except for a few small niche producers) builds models to compete directly with the leaders. Once you determine how the models of those companies fit your needs, you'll be able to shop other brands more intelligently.

If you're fortunate enough to find three or four brands that meet your needs, you are then in a position to start negotiating for the best price.

Bargains in folding trailers are available in most sections of the country, due to the fiercely competitive market environment. As outlined elsewhere in this book, the best bargains will be found in campers with eight-foot boxes.

7
RV TRENDS
AND CONSTRUCTION

Buying an RV that is being built and sold as part of a national trend is a great way to travel in the latest style, but it may not be the path to follow if you hope to make your purchase at the lowest possible price. Achieving savings by riding a trend depends almost entirely on timing. Ironically, bucking a trend also can cost you more -- or less -- depending upon how badly RV dealerships want to sell non-trend products.

During a trend's initial stage -- in reality, just *before* it comes to be recognized as a trend -- a newly emerging product's pricing often is quite attractive because both the manufacturer and its dealer network want to draw as much attention to it as possible. Typically, however, perceptive dealers recognize very quickly whether a new RV concept has an exceptional profit potential, and if that product also lacks strong competition, they have a tendency to boost prices as much as possible so they can earn good profits while demand is high and supply is low. Thus, there usually is only a brief opportunity to save money by riding the early stages of a trend.

A concept becomes a full trend, however, only when a variety of versions is offered. And, one fact of life within the RV field is that no trend can ever achieve its full potential until industry leader Fleetwood Enterprises incorporates it into its product lineup.

TRENDY BARGAINS

At the point where several competitors join the trend, the industry-wide pricing picture will begin to improve suddenly, and at that time, aggressive shoppers can usually ride the trend and find excellent bargains at the same time, taking advantage of fierce, broad-based competition for market share.

Periodically, RV manufacturers and dealers become so caught up pursuing business related to various trends that they neglect some types of non-trend products. At times like that, shoppers can find bargains in relatively unpopular models that are virtually being ignored in the trendy price wars. Dealers might even be ecstatic about moving those units off their lots in order to make room for faster-selling trend models. For example, as the trend toward fifth-wheels with single large slideouts became full-blown, dealers took every opportunity to dump models with two small slideouts. Some of the best bargains I've ever seen were made available in the early 1990s to shoppers who found reduced-price double-slide fivers appealing, despite common knowledge that those units would not have good long-term resale value.

Similarly, during the jump-on-the-bandwagon trend during 1999-2001 toward the new ultra-lightweight towables, some models of standard-construction travel trailers and fifth-wheels were neglected, and bargains quickly developed for those as dealers tried to move those units off their lots to make room for the lightweights.

The 2000 and 2001 model years also saw some excellent

bargains for large gasoline-fueled Class A motorhomes, in part because dealers and manufacturers were concentrating their efforts on trendy diesel pushers and in part because of escalating gasoline prices.

INNOVATION NOT TRENDY

Significantly, very few RV trends are closely related to innovative design or construction concepts. Four important exceptions to that were the creation of so-called *basement* motorhomes (pioneered by Fleetwood); development of large fifth-wheel slideouts; the trend toward wide-body RVs with innovative floorplans, and the late 1990s rebirth of lightweight towables. In each case, the trends were validated by Fleetwood's participation: In the case of the fifth-wheels, Fleetwood modified all its brands to feature single large slideouts, including its premium-priced Avion, and it subsequently added a Westport brand and a Savanna. Fleetwood joined the wide-body trend in a major way -- by converting its Tioga Arrow and Jamboree Rallye brands of mini-motorhomes to wide-bodies. And not until Fleetwood introduced its own lightweight towables was the trend toward those reborn vehicles fully validated.

At the same time, appearance of the Westport also underscored industry-wide acceptance of another trend -- toward upscale towables with a broad range of standard appointments and a framework of peripheral aluminum.

An important difference in the five trends was that four of them -- basement motorhomes, large slideouts, wide-body design and lightweight construction -- could be applied to a broad spectrum of price ranges, while the upscale, peripheral aluminum trend was focused almost entirely on the low end of the mid-price range. Most trends, in fact, follow the pattern of the upscale trailers and are limited to specific price levels. In addition, most trends are also little more than short-term marketing efforts that take advantage of shifts in consumer purchasing habits. Those shifts nearly always disappear after a few years, replaced by newer buying trends. An important characteristic of short-term trends is that they frequently reappear years after they've gone out of fashion. One of the best examples of this was the sudden, unexpected renewed popularity of front-kitchen travel trailers -- a floorplan that had been out of fashion for several years before re-emerging in the mid-1980s. Similarly, rear-kitchen fifth-wheels came back into vogue a few years ago after being unpopular for more than a decade, and Winnebago started a brief resurgence in production of small, inexpensive Class A motorhomes with its Warrior/Passage series several years after the industry had declared that type of coach dead and buried.

PRICE-SPECIFIC TRENDS

Price-specific trends of recent vintage include:
- Economy-priced eight-foot folding camping trailers.
- High-end, luxuriously equipped folding trailers.
- Fully equipped high-end pickup truck campers.
- Mid-size fifth-wheels with large slideouts.
- Fifth-wheels with stand-up space in front bedrooms.
- A new evolution away from small 16-20 foot travel trailers and toward mid-size models.
- Low-priced bus-style Class A motorhomes.

- •Relatively low priced Class A motorhomes with rear diesel engines.
- •Floorplan variations of the forward-facing sofa layout that Coachmen popularized with its wide-body motorhomes.
- •Family-oriented front-bedroom travel trailers.
- •Large low-cost mini-motorhomes of 28-30 feet.

In most cases, prices of RVs associated with trends fall when the trendy models become widely available and heavily stocked by dealerships. As dealerships frantically build their inventories with those models, the manufacturers that produce them frequently offer wholesale cost-cutting incentives to promote even faster stocking -- and those incentives cannot help but result in price reductions for retail customers who shop around aggressively.

As a direct result of the trends which developed during the mid-1990s, several types of bargains will continue to be available for a few years unless an economic recession occurs. The best bargains will be found in 26 to 29-foot travel trailers with front kitchens. Also look for good prices in fifth-wheels of 28 to 30 feet with large slideouts; wide-body RVs in the low to medium price ranges; 27 to 29-foot mini motorhomes with rear queen-size beds and L-shaped mid-coach galleys; entry-level bus-style Class A's of 26 to 28 feet; eight-foot folding camping trailers; camping vans with self-containment features; small, low-priced Class A's.

Anticipating future trends that are likely to affect RV prices is difficult, but not impossible, because the trends nearly always develop in response to needs of the marketplace. In 1995, the trend toward peripheral aluminum framing, for example, got a boost from an escalation in wood costs that made use of aluminum more economically viable. By 2000, the huge number of SUVs, light-duty pickup trucks and mini-vans on the highways helped the newly introduced lightweight towables succeed; that trend had been forecast for several years, but it simply took time to develop.

An analysis of the inventories at RV dealerships at any one point could indicate possible short-term trends in the near future. Based on cyclical consumer buying habits, it is not difficult to imagine that models in short supply now might have customers clamoring for them in a few more months. Going into the 2001 spring selling season, for example, inventory shortages existed for non-trend units such as mid-priced travel trailers with front living rooms.

For the last few years, industry analysts have predicted a boom in pickup truck campers as a direct response to the phenomenal sales of light trucks. But although truck caps *have* soared, the only real gain in pickup campers that has been seen was the result of Fleetwood's entering the field and filling its dealership pipeline with units that ultimately had to be retailed. Still, at some point, it seems reasonable to expect a major increase in demand for those campers...

RESULTS OF EARLIER TRENDS

By refining the trends in recreational vehicle design that began in the late 1980s, during the latter half of the 1990s, America's RV manufacturers moved into a new era of trailers and motorhomes that were not only more livable and functional, but also more affordable.

The result was an evolutionary type of RV that was both

shorter and wider than before; it had more living space than earlier models but was less expensive; it was more fully equipped but lighter in weight.

The two most important innovations of RV construction during the past dozen years -- jumbo slideouts and wide-body design -- have combined to encourage the development of models that feature more comfortable floorplans, larger bathrooms, more countertop space in kitchens and bathrooms, larger nightstands in bedrooms, and king-size beds and even walk-in closets! At the same time, important trends in RV framing and appliance redesign have enabled RV manufacturers to trim overall RV weights. Meanwhile, accessory *"packaging"* techniques have resulted in a complete restructuring of RV options and wholesale/retail pricing.

The culmination of all this innovation is seen most clearly in the 2001 models. Here are some of the features that are exciting RV buyers:

•Shorter fifth-wheels, some as small as 23 feet, with large slideouts.

•Mid-priced travel trailers with large slideout sections.

•Shorter wide-body motorhomes, travel trailers and fifth-wheels.

•Wide-body folding camping trailers.

•Folding trailers with slideout sections.

•Economy-priced hard-side travel trailers with folding trailer-type front and rear end bunks.

•A much broader selection of Class A motorhomes with slideout living room extensions.

•More Class C mini-motorhomes with slideouts.

•A broader selection of mid-size 25-foot-long Class C's

than has been available for many years.

•Increased emphasis on lightweight towables with smooth, laminated exterior sidewalls.

•More emphasis on diesel pusher motorhomes of 30 or 32 feet long. On the other hand, sales of large bus-style luxury motorhomes priced in the $200,000-$300,000 range hit a major snag during 2000-2001 because of unexpectedly high gasoline prices, and it's anybody's guess when -- or even if -- they will recover the market strength they enjoyed during the late 1990s.

•More models of fifth-wheels with triple slideouts (primarily rear-kitchen floorplans with one slideout on the door side) and even four slideouts.

To illustrate some of these developing trends, we need to look no farther than Airstream, one of the oldest RV companies in America and one that is famous for being quite careful about changes to its product line. In the late 1990s, that company switched production entirely to 101-inch wide-body trailers because of the improved livability they provide. Executives there also changed their thinking that motorhome slideouts were a fad, and Airstream Class A's now offer optional slideouts. Airstream also is focusing more strongly on mid-priced products.

Even folding camping trailers are wider. Viking Recreational Vehicles started that trend when it added six inches to the width of its units and then equipped them with longer bunks and improved interior livability such as larger dinettes and queen-size bunks. The 85-inch wide-body Vikings also were equipped with an axle and rubber suspension system that could be adjusted for different towing heights, thereby eliminating drop-hitches and making it easier for the campers to be towed by minivans and sports/utility vehicles.

I'll make my own prediction about a trend that I expect to see as a result of the high gasoline prices: a re-discovery and new emphasis on park model trailers of all types. This is one of those trendy phenomena that occurred in the past when gasoline supplies were tight. Consumers, not willing to give up their outdoor experiences, decided to travel less by spending their weekends and vacations in a single campground, and they created an enormous demand for leased and membership campsites on which they parked their RVs. An expanding market for park models resulted. I see the same type of demand developing currently as a reaction to the high gas prices, and that demand could become a full-fledged trend within months.

If that trend develops, look for several RV companies to leap back into production of park trailers. Demand for RV lots at membership and lease-type campgrounds will skyrocket, and a frantic, price-cutting competition will develop among RV dealers who handle the park trailers. While the park trailers remain trendy, excellent bargains will be available for consumers who shop around for them. But beware: The trend will fall apart as soon as gasoline prices decline significantly. Then both campsites and the used park trailers themselves will be widely available at -- you guessed it -- bargain prices!

8
BRAND CONSIDERATIONS

When you're shopping for either a new or used RV, brand names can be of critical importance. In some ways, they are even more important for the used-RV buyer than they are for someone who is planning to purchase a new RV. A new-RV buyer, for example, can be fairly confident that the vehicle he purchases was built by a manufacturer that is still in business; a used-RV buyer has no such assurance. Chances are good that replacement parts, if they are needed, are readily available for a family's new RV; the buyer of a used unit cannot make that assumption.

Unfortunately, unless you are familiar with brands and the histories of companies that manufacture RVs, discovering which brands to consider and which to avoid could prove difficult. Brand awareness is made even tougher by the fact that *some brand names suddenly disappear and then just as suddenly are revived*. A good case in point is the Mallard name. Originally, Mallard was a brand produced by Entwistle Corporation, a company which went out of business in the late 1970s. A few years later, the name was resurrected by a new corporation called the Mallard Coach Company. Despite enjoying several years of phenomenal growth, Mallard went bankrupt after its top executives moved on to other endeavors.

Then in 1994, the Mallard brand was revived by Fleetwood Industries and, within a few months, became one of the most popular brands of travel trailers in America again.

But the Mallard trailers produced by Entwistle had no real relationship to the trailers built by Mallard Coach, and neither the Entwistle nor the Mallard Coach units had relationship to the Fleetwood models. Parts, accessories, paint schemes, fabrics, construction methods -- none of those were necessarily interchangeable with the features of the new Fleetwood-built trailers. A family owning either an Entwistle or a Mallard Coach unit could not expect to buy replacement parts from any Fleetwood dealer handling the new Mallard brand.

The Mallards of Entwistle and Mallard Coach are what is referred to in the RV industry as *orphans*. Their manufacturers -- their parents -- do not exist any more. Not only are parts hard to find for an *orphaned* RV, but its resale value declines dramatically. I've seen cases in which the value of a $30,000 RV has declined to less than half that amount within a year after its manufacturer went out of business.

There are currently tens of thousands of *orphaned* RVs still being used and sold throughout the country. There are even some *new* orphan units for sale on dealers' lots, produced by manufacturers that closed their doors more recently. To help you identify the most popular orphan brands that are still in use, we've listed them in Appendix IV in the back of this book.

LEARNING ABOUT RV BRANDS

Prospective buyers *can* become self-educated about RV brands. Keep in mind, first of all, that the RV industry is quite close-knit, and stories about the successes and failures of manufacturers spread quite quickly through the nation's ranks of RV dealerships. Most dealers are quite happy to inform their prospective customers about the current difficulties being faced by competitive brands. They are seldom good sources of negative information about the brands that they stock and sell, of course.

Many veteran RVers also keep up to date with developments in the industry, and they are excellent sources for RV buyers to cultivate. In fact, I strongly recommend that an inexperienced camper seek suggestions from several camping acquaintances before buying a new or used RV. Friends of yours who are campers themselves probably can steer you toward the type and brand of unit that is most likely to fit your needs, based on their knowledge of your lifestyle.

Also, if your home computer is online, visit the popular RV-oriented chat lines and ask the enthusiasts there for their opinions; they won't hesitate to give them to you. One very popular RV chatline is through the public-access Usenet.com; another is Microsoft's new RV Lifestyle community (at http://communities.msn.com/RVLIFESTYLE. The RVAmerica website also has a very popular chatline that is worthwhile visiting. For others, check out our new book, *Camping on the Internet*, available directly from Cottage Publications or from Camping World for $14.95.

When considering RV brands, try to learn whether the brand is still being produced and whether its manufacturer is still in business. Remember, just because a brand's manufacturer is still operating does not guarantee that the brand itself is being built; old brands are being dropped constantly, and when they are, their parts and furnishings often are discontinued.

AVAILABILITY OF SERVICE

Because the availability of nation-wide repair service is important to an RVing family that travels extensively, a brand's widespread popularity can be quite valuable. There are numerous RV brands, however, that are popular in one section of the country and not in others. Several brands built in California and Oregon are virtually unknown in New England, for example, while some other brands that are well known in Ohio and Pennsylvania are simply not available on the West Coast.

Obviously, if Brand X is not stocked and sold by California dealers, a Californian who buys Brand X in Indiana and takes it home with him risks not being able to find replacement parts as well as being disappointed by the declining resale value of his unit.

Brand names also are quite important for another critical reason: The brand's reputation in the marketplace as a high-quality or low-quality product is a major factor in determining its resale value. Although sometimes a brand's reputation is not altogether deserved, *an RV's image in the marketplace is usually a fairly accurate gauge of its quality.* That does not necessarily mean a hot-selling RV is a high-quality one, however. Some of the best-selling brands in America today are quite poorly built but are sales leaders because of their low prices, not because of their quality. A few other brands with excellent, long-standing reputations for their quality may not, in actual fact, be well built any longer; I can think of some that have serious quality problems even though their high-quality image lives on.

Although generally speaking, the RV manufacturers with reputations for building quality products deserve them, sometimes those reputations extend to all their brands, even including ones that are built with less quality than the brands responsible for the quality image. Conversely, manufacturers that are burdened with reputations for poor quality nearly always find it difficult to break out of that mold, even when they produce expensive, high-quality vehicles.

QUESTIONS TO ASK

When considering a particular brand seriously, here are some questions that should be answered by well-informed friends, the dealer handling the brand, and that dealer's competitors:

- What is the brand's reputation for quality?
- What is the dealership's reputation for honesty and service work?
- Do models of the brand consistently need servicing and warranty repair?
- How cooperative are the dealer and the manufacturer in performing warranty service?
- Is the RV difficult to repair because of the way it is built or the materials used to build it?
- Is the dealership capable of repairing it, even if serious body work is necessary?
- Under what circumstances will the RV have to be returned to the factory for service?
- Are replacement parts readily available?
- How long have the dealership and the manufacturer been in business?
- How extensively in America is the brand distributed?
- How many dealers sell and service the brand, and is a list

of those dealers available (most manufacturers do not make public the names and locations of their franchised dealerships)?

•Is the brand still being produced?

Special consideration should be given to the brand's resale value. For that information, do not depend upon what the dealer tells you. Go to your library and check the brand's history in the *Kelley Blue Book* or *NADA Recreational Vehicle Appraisal Guide*. Determine how values of the brand have depreciated in other years compared with the values of competitive brands. Also, do some price-comparing by learning the asking prices of used models currently offered for sale throughout your community. The sale prices of five-year-old units can give you a clear picture of how rapidly values decline on the brand that interests you.

No discussion about RV brands would be complete without at least some mention of those that are custom-built and sold directly to retail customers instead of through dealerships. There is a wide variety of reasons why RV travelers want or need custom-designed RVs, but in virtually all cases, special needs dictate the purchase of RVs with unusual floorplans or furnishings. As might be expected, the most common reason for ordering a custom unit is for full-time living. Many adventurous couples planning to hit the road full time insist upon doing it with exactly the right rig to fit their lifestyles, their living habits, their travel preferences and, most importantly, their budgets.

RV travelers who are physically handicapped also are good

customers of the custom-builders. Generally, they want RVs with wider aisles, larger bathrooms that are specially equipped, wheelchair lift systems, lower countertops and perhaps even customized driving compartments. Traveling salesmen, clergymen, sportsmen and even entertainers have their own special travel and living needs, and custom-builders offer them the opportunity to own RVs that are designed with individual character. Others want specialized rigs for trips to Alaska, Mexico, Europe, South America or Australia. I have several writer friends who travel extensively while they're researching and writing magazine articles and books, and they require office space where they can store resource books and research material in addition to a work area large enough for a desk, computer, printer and telephone/facsimile machine. Hobbyists such as antique collectors, rockhounds and animal trainers have their own special needs, and customized RVs can provide them with the kinds of space that meet those needs.

During our many years of participation in the RVing lifestyle, we've heard endless reasons why people order RVs custom-built. Perhaps the most intriguing of those was given by a man who bought a custom-built travel trailer from Travel Units of Elkhart, Indiana, several years ago. His wife was quite short and, as might be expected, the couple ordered a trailer with lowered countertops and cabinets throughout.

However, the trailer also had a huge, full-width closet across the rear, in the bedroom, and featured a standard rear window at the back of the closet. Puzzled, we asked the husband why they had designed a trailer with a window that had no apparent value. Somewhat embarrassed, the man answered, "My wife is very nosy, and she likes to know what her neighbors are doing. With that window, she can stand inside the closet and look outside without alerting the neighbors that she's spying on them."

CUSTOMER IS ALWAYS RIGHT

Like all custom-builders of RVs, Sam Paolillo, the owner of Travel Units, has heard thousands of strange reasons why people want travel trailers or fifth-wheels created to fit their particular tastes. But except for making sure he understands what his customers want, he never questions their motives. His company's policy is that the customer is always right -- no matter how strange their requests seem to be.

Paolillo creates several dozen custom-designed coaches each year, and each one is an original unit built to order. Historically, Travel Units focused its primary attention on travel trailers, but in recent years most of his customers have ordered fifth-wheels.

Elsewhere in the Midwest, Spacecraft Motor Homes of Concordia, Missouri, has earned a highly respected reputation for its custom-built fifth-wheels, but the company also made its mark on the RV industry by becoming the first manufacturer to offer Class A motorhomes with power slideout sections. Travel Supreme, Newmar Corporation and Carriage, Inc., three In-diana competitors that are highly respected for their luxury-class fifth-wheels, respond quite often to their customers' re-quests for specialized trailers, and Newmar has even branched out into customized Class A motorhomes in recent years.

All five of those companies compete for the same types of

buyers -- primarily full-time RVers and professional people who travel all year -- and they all emphasize personal, direct contact with their customers. While Travel Supreme, Newmar and Carriage require that actual purchases be handled by their franchised dealers, however, Travel Units and Spacecraft are among the few American RV companies today that have no dealer networks and handle nothing except custom orders.

Paolillo's conservatively designed trailers tend to attract customers who want high-quality furnishings at the lowest-possible price; the fifth-wheels and motorhomes built by Spacecraft have strong appeal for travelers who insist upon one-of-a-kind vehicles that range from merely distinctive to truly outrageous. Some of Spacecraft's units are built with multiple slideouts, including power sections on the non-traditional curbside, and the company's fifth-wheels and motorhomes have such distinctive exterior shapes that they are impossible to mistake for any other brand.

Probably the epitome of custom RV design, however, comes from a little-known company in Columbus, Ohio, that is quite appropriately named Custom Coach Corporation. That firm specializes in custom-converting transit bus shells for private use, and its *motorcoaches* sell for between $300,000 and $1.3 million or more! They are, without question, the most luxurious RVs on the road. Custom Coach has built a strong following among well known entertainers. Its customer list, in fact, is a who's who in the country and rock music fields. Personalities such as Loretta Lynn and Mel Tillis are repeat buyers of Custom Coach buses, and the popularity of the company's conversions also extends into various branches of sports competition, including the nation's top golfers, boxers and tennis players.

RVers who are not quite so luxury-oriented might prefer to order a custom-built pickup truck camper, mini-motorhome or van camper instead. Alaskan/USA of North Bend, Washington, has a long history of building high-end truck campers to fit any customer's desires. Born Free MotorCoach of Iowa and Lazy Daze of California are probably the best-known producers of customer-direct minis, although Lazy Daze tries to build its units within a framework of specific floorplans. Among the custom producers of van campers, Sportsmobile and Coach House have excellent reputations for their quality units. Several other RV manufacturers -- including Airstream, Teton Homes, Lance Camper Manufacturing Corporation and a broad range of companies that produce luxury motorhomes -- also are happy to work with customers on developing units that fit special needs.

CREATE YOUR OWN RV

No matter which company is chosen for the job, the procedure for giving birth to a custom recreational vehicle follows one of two avenues:

ONE -- The buyer contacts the manufacturer directly and then either meets personally with a design specialist or orders the unit designed and built long-distance utilizing the mail and telephones.

TWO -- The buyer works directly in the field with a franchised dealership that handles the specific brand of RV that is desired. In this case, the buyer conveys his wishes to the dealer, who actually places the order and arranges for all special work to be done.

Both systems work quite well, but companies which specialize in custom work claim their customers are more fully satisfied if the designer and the buyer can meet and work out details together. "The customer needs to understand our philosophy about custom work, and we need to learn all we can about how the customer lives and travels," a Midwest design specialist said.

In either case, it is wise to plan at least one visit to the factory while construction is in process. Subtle changes can usually be made at such time without causing much, if any, impact upon price, and potential misunderstandings between the manufacturer and the customer can be resolved early. Several custom builders such as Newell Coach Corporation of Miami, Oklahoma, require customer visits as part of the procedure. In fact, that company insists its customers pick up their new coaches at the factory and spend a few days in them, on-site, before the sales transaction is considered completed.

ADVANTAGES OF CUSTOM WORK

Buying a custom-built RV is not necessarily expensive. Several custom builders insist their products cost about the same as the customer would pay for similarly equipped *stock* units on any RV dealer's sales lot.

One obvious advantage in buying a custom unit is that virtually every appliance and accessory can be selected by the RVer; thus, if the buyer wants specific brands of microwave, furnace, air conditioner or awning, he can be assured he will get those with his new rig. However, he might pay slightly more for that flexibility than standard stock furnishings would cost him if he ordered a new RV from a high-volume manufacturer.

I do not know of any custom builder that is not willing to work closely with customers in order to hold down costs.

Typically, each custom builder has special relationships with certain appliance vendors and other accessory suppliers, and costs can be controlled somewhat by allowing the manufacturer to order equipment available at the best prices. If it does not matter to you whether your RV refrigerator is a Dometic or a Norcold, for example, the manufacturer probably can save you money by installing the refrigerator brand he can buy at the lowest price, depending upon his business relationship with the refrigerator vendors.

Significant cost variables also exist in the areas of frame size, type and thickness of exterior skin, and the selection of countertops, flooring, floor coverings, cabinet frames and doors, tire quality, interior and exterior lighting, furniture upholstery, axle strength and even the hardware on the drawers and cabinet doors.

A POSSIBLE DISADVANTAGE

One potential disadvantage to buying an RV directly from the factory where it is built is in the method of handling service and warranty claims. Because those manufacturers have no franchised dealer network, you must either return the RV to the factory to have warranty work done or you will have to find a service center willing to repair an RV it did not sell. Custom manufacturers with good reputations generally have no difficulty in finding service centers to handle warranty work, but even so, lack of an in-place dealer network is a shortcoming that should be considered by someone who intends to travel extensively.

If you are considering buying a custom-built RV, here is the procedure we recommend you follow:

ONE -- Decide which type or types of RVs you want to own, and then write to the manufacturers which specialize in those types. Ask for literature about the company and its products; a list of customer references, including telephone numbers; an outline of pricing policies, and a clear explanation of how the company typically works with its customers.

TWO -- Plan a personal tour of the plant where your RV would be built. Even if the design phase will be handled by working with a franchised dealer, you should be familiar with the plant and personnel where the construction work will be done.

THREE -- Check the company's references, making sure that earlier buyers were satisfied not only with the RVs they bought, but also with follow-up service and repair work. The lifeblood of all custom builders is the good will they have with their customers, and if a manufacturer is not performing satisfactorily, those customers probably will know about it.

FOUR -- Make certain you know exactly how future repair work -- and especially warranty repairs -- will be handled. That is, must the RV be returned to the factory for work or can repairs be made by an extensive list of independent service centers.

FIVE -- Ask questions. Learn about prospective manufacturers' storage spaces, frame and construction techniques, general weights and recommended payload capacities, hitch and tow vehicle requirements (if buying a trailer), chassis and engine alternatives (if buying a motorhome), financial arrangements required, typical exterior and interior dimensions, insulation.

Finally, ask whether the company is a member of RVIA (the Recreation Vehicle Industry Association). Although RVIA membership does not guarantee you the company does quality work or serves its customers honestly, it does mean that its products are inspected periodically for safety (wiring, venting, drainage, etc.).

9
COMPLETING YOUR PURCHASE

So now you're ready to buy your new RV. Or are you?

If you have any doubts, now is the time for putting them to rest. Are the brand and model you've selected the best ones for your family and your camping lifestyle? To make certain they are -- or at least, to lessen your doubts -- you have two final steps to take:

ONE -- Before you pay even a small deposit for the unit, you should check it out more thoroughly for potential short-comings, and you should take it out for a test drive or a tow-test.

TWO -- You should investigate the availability and prices of insurance and financing to make certain the *whole* cost of the RV is considered as part of your family's budget.

That final check-out should be much more exacting than the brief examination you gave to the unit when you first went RV shopping -- especially if the RV you are considering is a used one. Even new RVs are quite likely to have problems, and your first camping outing will prove to be much more enjoy-able if you can learn about those problems and have them corrected before you take the unit camping. I have always maintained -- and I repeat it at every opportunity -- that the perfect recreational vehicle has never been built!

DON'T ASSUME IT'S OKAY

I cannot help but recall the first travel trailer my family and I tested back in the early 1970s. We drove to the factory where it was being built in order to pick it up, but we arrived just before it rolled off the assembly line. As we watched it being finished, two workers placed the plastic water tank under the sofa and connected it to water lines. In the process, one of them broke the nearby water pump switch. His co-worker mentioned the broken switch to him, and he replied, "Let it go. The dealer will fix it."

Later, I learned that what I had seen was not an isolated incident; RV line workers at too many plants, preoccupied with high-volume production and insensitive to their companies' demands for quality, tended to shrug off shortcomings they regarded as minor, especially since they knew that dealerships buying the units would make any necessary repairs. After that, I tried to make certain every RV I tested was thoroughly checked before I took it camping. But time after time, I found myself in an isolated campground with a furnace that would not operate, a water heater that would not light, LP-gas lines that leaked and toilets that would not flush!

My best advice to an RV buyer, therefore, is never to assume that anything on a new or used RV operates correctly until you've checked it personally.

As part of your final pre-purchase check-out, review your initial impressions of the RV as recorded on your shopping Features Checklist and your Impressions Checklist (Appendixes I and III in the back of this book). On the items you listed as "Fair" on the Features Checklist, consider why you did not give them higher ratings and determine whether repairs or replacements are necessary. Remember, at this point in your buying process, you should be prepared to purchase the unit, but the seller should be aware you will not actually hand over any money until you are satisfied with the RV's performance. As a committed buyer, it is your right to demand that the operation of an appliance be demonstrated, for example, even if that means the seller must go to the trouble of filling an empty propane tank or connecting the unit to electricity and water.

On the Impressions Checklist, if you gave the RV you are considering seriously low marks in one or more areas, maybe you ought to reconsider whether it is the right RV for you and your lifestyle.

A FINAL INSPECTION

Your final inspection should involve four areas:

•A personal walk-through and examination of the unit for damage, workmanship errors and leaks.

•Demonstration by the seller of appliances and accessories.

•Actual operation of the appliances.

•Determination that all electrical outlets are operating and that their polarity is correct.

Keep in mind that demonstrating appliance operation is not simply a matter of flicking a switch and observing them operating. The refrigerator, for example, must be allowed to cool for at least a couple of hours; the water heater must be filled with water, supplied with LP-gas and given time to heat the water. Therefore, we suggest asking the seller to prepare the appliances for demonstration and then allowing several hours or a full day for the appliances to operate prior to being demonstrated.

SPECIAL CAUTIONS

We have provided a checklist (see Appendix II, Pre-Purchase Checklist) in the back of this book for you to use, but you need to be aware of some special points first. For example, in making sure the refrigerator operates properly, you should ask the seller to operate it with electricity, but also open the outside of the compartment and let you verify that, when on LP-gas, the gas flame igniter works. The seller also should show you how to adjust the temperature controls of the refrigerator, water heater and air conditioner. In demonstrating the sanitary sewer system, the seller should actually remove the sewer line cap and open the valves so that you can verify they are not corroded in place. Details of the systems monitor panel should be explained. Not only should a generator be operated, but its external start switch and its routine servicing requirements should also be explained. The seller should show you not only how to light the range and oven, but also how to use pilot lights. Unusual features of a microwave oven and an air conditioner should be demonstrated.

It is critical that the polarity of each electrical outlet be checked. Reverse polarity in an RV can kill you! If you are buying the RV from an individual, invest $10 for a plug-in device that checks polarity. If you are doing business with a dealership, ask the sales person to check the rig's polarity with you present. Reverse polarity rarely occurs, but during the 30 years we've camped in RVs, we've seen it in three different units.

As part of the check-out procedure, you should make certain that operating manuals for all appliances and accessories are provided; that literature about the model you are purchasing is given to you (it will list options you might want to consider buying later), and that full warranty papers are explained and furnished. Also ask the dealer about his service and repair facilities: hours his shop is open, which brands of appliances the shop is authorized to service, whether the shop can handle major damage repairs and mechanical service, whether it does routine maintenance and winterizing, hourly service rates and flat charges for routine work.

Every RV -- new or used -- should be road-tested before it is purchased. When buying a trailer, it is important to tow-test it with your own personal vehicle, if possible. That allows you to learn exactly how your whole rig will perform as a unit. If your tow vehicle is not available, ask the dealer to provide one; most dealers will oblige.

If you have not towed extensively, keep in mind that the connected rig probably consists of a 25 to 30-foot-long trailer plus 15 to 18 feet of tow vehicle and that the trailer is about eight feet wide. Because of the trailer's size and the fact that it will cut across slightly and not follow exactly in the patch of the tow vehicle, turns must be a little wider than with a solo truck or automobile. Apply brakes with various amounts of pressure to ensure that the trailer brakes operate properly in conjunction with the tow vehicle's; most trailerists prefer a trailer's brakes to engage a moment before those of the tow vehicle.

How well are you able to handle the rig in traffic? Can you judge distance adequately, using only the two side mirrors of the tow vehicle? Does the acceleration lag bother you seriously? Does the drag of the trailer make towing it too uncomfortable for you? Does it sway or tail-wag in spite of sway control devices? How quickly does it stop when you apply the brakes.

When test-driving a motorhome, check how it handles, its turning radius, cornering, front and rear stability, front end bounce, throttle noise, engine knock, exhaust smoke, whether the cab seats are comfortable and whether you have a clear view of the speedometer and other sections of the instrument panel. Are there bothersome rattles from the windows, range, range hood? Is there any lag in pickup? How good is the visibility out the rear window and through the side mirrors? How does it perform at highway speeds? Do cross-winds cause it to handle poorly? How responsive is it when backing? Will you have difficulty parking it at a narrow campsite?

If, after the tow-test and your final check-out, you are uncertain whether you should invest in the RV, consider asking the seller to let you use it overnight. The seller might require a deposit in order to permit you to use the unit, but you should get a statement in writing from him that your deposit will be returned if you decide not to buy the RV.

Most RV buyers do not realize it, but the manner in which an RV is purchased can be used as a bargaining tool by the astute shopper. And I'm not referring here to offering cold, hard cash to a dealer in exchange for a reduced price! The vast majority of all RV loans -- about two thirds -- involve financing arranged by RV dealerships. Part of the reason for that is that dealers collect fees from lenders for arranging financing, but equally important is the fact that dealers' involvement takes most of the legwork out of searching for loan rates and terms.

While shopping around for an RV, a prospective buyer also should learn as much as possible about the financing plans that are available through competing dealerships. Frequently, the deciding factor when negotiating a purchase between two or more dealerships could come down to which one can offer the best payment terms or interest rates. Most dealers have at least a couple of different financing sources, and agreements between the dealers and the lenders are so widely varied, and in some cases so complicated, that they cannot be outlined here except to emphasize that dealers sometimes have a great deal of latitude in arranging loans for their customers.

That does not mean a buyer should not arrange his own financing through a bank, credit union or savings and loan association. But I recommend keeping all options open, especially if a closely negotiated deal in the end hinges upon the amount of a down payment or lower interest rates.

Down payments of 15-20% are usually required in direct financing programs with the buyer's lender, although smaller down payments can often be negotiated when home equity loans are used in the purchase. Indirect, dealer-arranged loans are available with down payments of 10-20%, and even though the lender pays the dealership a middle-man's fee, a dealer-arranged loan is not necessarily more expensive than a personally arranged one. Payment terms for both types of loan are typically 60-120 months, with home equity payouts for luxury-class motorhomes sometimes being available for up to 180 months.

Another reason to shop around for financing is that some lenders base their rates upon the interest being charged locally for used car loans, while other lenders use home mortgage rates as a guide. In any case, the Internal Revenue Service regards self-contained RVs as second homes, and so interest payments for them are tax-deductible.

Keep in mind when shopping for financing that loans on RVs are regarded quite positively by most lenders, not only because they are very profitable, but also because they have an extremely low default rate.

RV buyers also should shop around for insurance coverage, although most purchasers do not. Substantial savings can be realized by comparing rates after asking from quotes from numerous sources. Owners of motorhomes are particularly vulnerable to paying high insurance rates, partly because of the cost of their coaches, but also because motorhomes are regarded as automotive-type vehicles and are subject to the same state insurance laws as cars and trucks.

There are four types of coverage applicable to RVs: personal property insurance, personal liability coverage, collision insurance and comprehensive coverage.

For most RVing families, loss of the personal property that they carry with them in their RVs already is covered by their homeowner's or renter's policy, so it is not necessary to add separate coverage. For full-time RVers who do not have a permanent home, a personal property floater can be added to other vehicle insurance at a very low rate -- perhaps $50 per year.

Personal liability insurance is not necessary for owners of towable RVs because they are already covered by liability provisions of their tow vehicle insurance. Motorhome owners do not have that automatic coverage, of course, and in most states, they are required to purchase liability insurance as well as personal injury coverage.

Collision insurance, which covers the RV in a collision or a rollover incident, is necessary for both towable and motorized RVs and, in most cases, collision coverage is purchased along with a comprehensive policy which covers a wide range of other incidents such as theft, hail damage, fire damage and vandalism. For the towables owner, the annual cost of collision and comprehensive insurance can range from $50 to $300. Full motorhome coverage, on the other hand, ranges from $500 to $2,000 per year. Additional premiums may be required to insure items such as coin collections, paintings and special jewelry. Some insurers suspend charges for partial coverage during periods when the RV is stored.

When shopping for insurance, ask for premium quotes from many different companies, both local and national.

Appendix I
Features Checklist

RV BRAND _____ YEAR _____

MANUFACTURER _____ DEALER _____

SALES PERSON'S NAME _____ DATE _____

LIVING ROOM.
     ___Sofa   ___Sofa/bed   ___Gaucho
     ___Cabinet bunk   ___Sidewall overhead cabinets
     Seating for all family members?   ___Yes ___No
Seating comfort: ___Excellent   ___Good   ___Poor
Rate lighting: ___Excellent   ___Good   ___Poor
     Living room floor carpeted?   ___Yes   ___No
     Window treatment type _____
     Window type _____
     ___TV antenna   ___Radio   ___Space for TV

KITCHEN.
     Type of sink _____   ___Water purifier
     ___Range   ___Range hood   ___Exhaust fan
     ___Oven   ___Coffeemaker   ___Pantry
     ___Microwave oven   ___Microwave/convection oven
     ___Booth dinette/bunk   ___Freestanding dinette
     ___Water pump switch   ___Water heater switch
     ___Power roof vent   ___Systems monitor panel
     Refrigerator size _____
     ___LP-gas   ___Electric   ___Gas/electric
Rate drawers: ___Excellent   ___Good   ___Poor
Rate storage: ___Excellent   ___Good   ___Poor
Rate lighting: ___Excellent   ___Good   ___Poor
Dining Space: ___Excellent   ___Good   ___Poor
Countertop space: ___Excellent   ___Good   ___Poor

BATHROOM.
     ___Shower   ___Tub   ___Toilet   ___Sink
     ___Shower curtain   ___Sliding shower door
     ___Linen storage   ___Laundry space
     ___Wall mirror   ___Medicine cabinet mirror
     ___Mirror on outside of bathroom door

___Towel bars/hooks   ___Heating duct

Rate shower/tub: ___Excellent   ___Good   ___Poor
Rate countertop: ___Excellent   ___Good   ___Poor
Rate lighting: ___Excellent   ___Good   ___Poor
Medicine cabinet: ___Excellent   ___Good   ___Poor
Rate storage: ___Excellent   ___Good   ___Poor
Toilet location: ___Excellent   ___Good   ___Poor

Type & brand of toilet _____
___Water pump switch   ___Extra sink in hallway

BEDROOM.

Type of bed(s) _____
Type of windows _____
Window treatment _____
___Overhead cabinets   ___Shirt closet(s)
___Nightstands   ___Underbed storage
___TV shelf or compartment   ___Privacy door
___Reading lights   ___Vanity area

Rate bed comfort: ___Excellent   ___Good   ___Poor
Rate storage: ___Excellent   ___Good   ___Poor
Rate lighting: ___Excellent   ___Good   ___Poor
Rate ventilation: ___Excellent   ___Good   ___Poor

OTHER FEATURES.

Sleeping capacity _____   Mealtime capacity _____
___In-floor ducted heat   ___Match-lighted furnace
___Roof rack & Ladder   ___LP-gas regulator
Water heater: ___LP-gas   ___Electric   ___Gas/electric
Water capacity of water heater _____
Type of air conditioner _____ BTU___
___Power converter   Amps___
___Generator   Brand _____   KW___
___Awning   ___Roof pod   ___Vacuum
___Cable TV jack   ___Water heater by-pass kit
___Icemaker   ___Washer/dryer
___Trailer hitch (motorhome)   ___Safety chains (trailer)
___Stabilizer jacks   ___Deadbolt lock   ___Screendoor

Rate water tank size: ___Excellent   ___Good   ___Poor
Rate holding tanks: ___Excellent   ___Good   ___Poor
Rate exterior storage: ___Excellent   ___Good   ___Poor
Rate exterior lighting: ___Excellent   ___Good   ___Poor
Exterior appearance: ___Excellent   ___Good   ___Poor

Interior livability:	___Excellent	___Good	___Poor
Rate fabrics:	___Excellent	___Good	___Poor
Rate interior decor:	___Excellent	___Good	___Poor
Rate electric outlets:	___Excellent	___Good	___Poor

Frame construction type _____ Insulation type_____
Exterior skin _____

List other needed features / negative features:

_____

_____

Appendix II
Pre-Purchase Checklist

As part of a final inspection of the RV you are ready to buy, use this list to verify whether or not features of the RV are operating and if any need to be repaired or replaced. As outline in Chapter 9, the final inspection should involve four areas:

1. Look for damage, workmanship errors and leaks.
2. Have all appliances and accessories demonstrated.
3. Actually operate all appliances.
4. Determine that all electrical outlets are operating and their polarity is correct.

APPLIANCES:

_____ Light furnace
_____ Light water heater
_____ Operate refrigerator
_____ Operate air conditioner
_____ Flush toilet
_____ Operate microwave oven
_____ Operate icemaker
_____ Operate leveling jacks (if motorhome)

SELLER SHOULD DEMONSTRATE:

_____ How to light water heater
_____ How to operate furnace
_____ How to operate refrigerator
_____ How to operate air conditioner
_____ Where water pump switch is located
_____ How to operate TV antenna
_____ How to operate holding tank drains
_____ How to operate convertible bunks
_____ How to light range pilot light
_____ How to light oven
_____ How to operate microwave
_____ How systems monitor panel operates
_____ How to replace water purifier
_____ How to operate windows
_____ How to start/service generator
_____ How LP-gas tanks/regulator operate

SELLER SHOULD PROVIDE:

_____ Appliances/accessories operating manuals
_____ Manufacturer's literature about the RV

INSPECT FOR WORKMANSHIP OR DAMAGE:

_____ Door hinges and latches
_____ Under drawers
_____ Inside cabinets, including corners
_____ Struts on lift-up beds
_____ Frames of beds

LOOK FOR:

_____ Rough corners or edges
_____ Screw heads protruding from heating ducts
_____ Sidewall delamination or buckling
_____ Dents, scratches
_____ Cracks in shower/tub
_____ Damaged screendoor
_____ Leaks
_____ Floor-level water lines inside cabinets
_____ LP-gas lines (smell for odor of rotten eggs)
_____ Check lines in outside storage areas
_____ Check ceiling for evidence of roof leaks

SELLER SHOULD REPLACE:

_____ Any damaged mirror
_____ Shower curtain
_____ Broken/burned out lightbulbs
_____ Inoperable struts on lift-up beds
_____ Other

Appendix III
Impressions Checklist

Using either a 10-scale or a 5-scale, rate each of the RV types, brands and models that interest you most. Make copies of this checklist and use the following criteria for measuring your impressions of each unit.

_____ Price

_____ Quality

_____ Serviceability

_____ Resale value

_____ Performance (towability or handling)

_____ Construction

_____ Equipment and features

_____ Floorplan (including sleeping space)

_____ Storage space

_____ Reputation and reliability of the dealership

_____ Reputation of the manufacturer

_____ Weight

_____ How the RV seems to fit your needs (for weekends, vacations, long or short trips, seasonally, off-road boondocking, long-term or full-time living)

_____ **TOTAL POINTS**

RV BRAND _____ RV TYPE _____

MODEL YEAR _____ MANUFACTURER _____

DEALERSHIP _____

SALES PERSON'S NAME _____ DATE _____

Appendix IV
Orphaned Brands

Here are some of the most popular RV brands that are no longer being built. We call such brands *"orphans."* Be careful about buying an *"orphan"* because parts and furnishings are usually not readily available for them.

Apeco	Apollo
Apache	Arabian
Avco	Banner
Bonanza	Blazon
Brougham	Champion
Conestoga	Country Squire
Cree	Diamond
Dutch Craft	Elkhart Traveler
Establishment	Fan
Fireball	Frolic
Go-Tag-A-Long	Granville
Heritage	Honey
Kings Highway	Landau
Legend	Leisure Time
Le Sharo	Marque
Marauder	Mayflower
Midas	Mobile Scout
Mobile Traveler	Mobile Villa
Monitor	Motoroam
Nimrod	Open Road
Perris Valley	Prairie Schooner
Ramblette	Rancho
Rawhide	Robinhood
Sports King	Sprinter
Suncrest	Swiss Colony
Titan	Tran Star
Traveleze	Travco
Travel Villa	Vacationeer
Vega	Venture
WideWorld	

Appendix V
Where and when to find RV bargains

State	Best for RV Bargains	Type of RV	Special bargains
AL	November-December	All types	Snowbird towables
AK	November-February	All types	Folding trailers
AR	November-December	All types	Snowbird towables
NC	November-December	All types	Folding trailers
SC	December-January	All types	Class A's
CO	November-January	All types	Truck campers
CT	November-December	All types	Small towables
FL	September & December	Towables	Park models
GA	September & December	Towables	Folding trailers
ID	November-February	All types	Fifth-wheels
IL	November-December	All types	Snowbird towables
IN	November-December	All types	Snowbird towables
IA	November-January	All types	Fifth-wheels
KS	November-January	Towables	Fifth-wheels
KY	December-January	Towables	Folding trailers
ME	November-December	All types	Small towables
MD	December	Towables	Folding trailers
MA	November-December	All types	Small towables
MI	November-December	All types	Snowbird towables
MN	December-January	All types	Folding trailers
MO	December-January	All types	Snowbird towables
MT	November-December	Towables	Fifth-wheels
NE	December-January	Towables	Fifth-wheels
NV	September & December	All types	Class A's
NH	December-January	Towables	Small towables
NJ	December-January	Motorhomes	Folding trailers
NY	December-January	Small RVs	Folding trailers
NM	November-December	Towables	Fifth-wheels
ND	December-January	All types	Snowbird towables
NC	November-December	All types	Towables
OH	November-December	All types	Snowbird towables
OK	December-January	Towables	Fifth-wheels
OR	November-January	All types	Class A's
PA	December-January	All types	Park Models
SC	November-December	All types	Towables
SD	December-January	All types	Snowbird towables
TN	December	All types	Folding trailers
TX	December-January	All types	Fifth-wheels
UT	December-January	Towables	Truck campers
VT	December-January	Towables	Small towables
VA	December-January	All types	Folding trailers

WA	November-December	All types	Fifth-wheels
WV	December-January	All types	Folding trailers
WI	November-December	All types	Folding trailers
WY	November-December	Towables	Fifth-wheels

NOTES

NOTES

NOTES

NOTES

NOTES